Grade 6

Reading & Math Practice

200 Teacher-Approved Practice Pages
to Build Essential Skills

New York • Toronto • London • Auckland • Sydney
Mexico City • New Delhi • Hong Kong • Buenos Aires

Teaching *Resources*

Contents

Cover design: Scott Davis
Interior design: Adrienne Downey, Melinda Belter, and Sydney Wright
Interior illustrations: Teresa Anderko, Maxie Chambliss, Steve Cox, Rusty Fletcher, Mike Gordon,
James Graham Hale, and Sydney Wright © Scholastic Inc.

Image credits: page 24 © Haven/iStockphoto; page 28 © NHPA/Superstock, Inc.; page 32 © Juanmonino/iStockphoto;
page 48 © Hank Shiffman/Bigstock; page 56 © Waterman Company/Corbis; page 60 © peruviano/Bigstock;
page 64 © Imagno/Getty Images; pages 104, 132, 144, and 196 © Bettmann/Corbis; page 184: Shi Yali/Bigstock

ISBN: 978-0-545-67262-7
Written by Marcia Miller and Martin Lee.
Copyright © 2014 by Scholastic Inc.
All rights reserved. Printed in the U.S.A.
Published by Scholastic Inc.

1 2 3 4 5 6 7 8 9 10   14   21 20 19 18 17 16 15 14

Introduction

Welcome!

Reading & Math Practice: Grade 6 is the perfect way to support the learning your child needs to soar in school and beyond. The colorful, fun, and engaging activity pages in this book will give your child plenty of opportunities to practice the important reading and math skills sixth graders are expected to master. These teacher-approved practice pages are a great way to help your child:

- ☑ reinforce key academic skills and concepts
- ☑ meet curriculum standards
- ☑ prepare for standardized tests
- ☑ succeed in school
- ☑ become a lifelong learner!

Research shows that independent practice helps children gain mastery of essential skills. Each set of practice pages contains a collection of activities designed to review and reinforce a range of skills and concepts. The consistent format will help your child work independently and with confidence. Skills include:

Reading & Language Arts	Math
Word Study	Place Value
Vocabulary	Multiplication & Division
Grammar	Fractions & Decimals
Reading Comprehension	Logic & Critical Thinking
Spelling	Solving Word Problems
	Interpreting Charts & Graphs

Turn the page for information about how these exercises will help your child meet the College and Career Readiness Standards for reading, language, and mathematics. Page 5 offers suggestions for introducing the practice pages to your child along with helpful tips for making the experience go smoothly. Pages 6–9 provide a close-up look at the features in each set of practice pages.

We hope you enjoy doing the activities in this book with your child. Your involvement will help make this a valuable educational experience and will support and enhance your child's learning!

Connections to the College and Career Readiness Standards

The standards for College and Career Readiness (CCR) serve as the backbone for the practice pages in this book. These broad standards were developed to establish educational expectations meant to provide students nationwide with a quality education that prepares them for college and careers. The following lists show how the activities in this book align with the standards in key areas of focus for students in grade 6.

Standards for English Language Arts	Standards for Mathematics
Reading Standards (Literary and Informational Texts)	**Mathematical Practice**
• Key Ideas and Details • Craft and Structure • Integration of Knowledge and Ideas • Range of Reading Level and Text Complexity	1. Make sense of problems and persevere in solving them. 2. Reason abstractly and quantitatively. 3. Construct viable arguments and critique the reasoning of others. 4. Model with mathematics. 5. Use appropriate tools strategically. 6. Attend to precision. 7. Look for and make use of structure. 8. Look for and express regularity in repeating reasoning.
Language	
• Conventions of Standard English • Knowledge of Language • Vocabulary Acquisition and Use	

Reading & Math Practice, Grade 6 © 2014 Scholastic Inc.

Getting Started

Each practice packet consists of two double-sided pages—one for reading followed by one for math. Introduce the packet to your child by going through the directions and walking through its features. Point out that activities in each section focus on different kinds of skills, and that the same features repeat throughout, always in the same order and position. In general, the practice pages progress in difficulty level and build on skills covered on previous pages. See pages 6–9 for more information.

Helpful Tips

★ For ease of use, gently tear out the pages your child will be working on along the perforated edges.

★ Invite your child to complete each packet over the course of a week, doing two or three exercises on a practice page each day.

★ If desired, allow your child to choose the order in which he or she will complete the exercises on the practice pages.

★ You'll find an answer key for each practice page, beginning on page 211. Review the answers together and encourage your child to share the thinking behind his or her answers.

★ Support your child's efforts and offer help when needed.

★ Display your child's work and share his or her progress with family and friends!

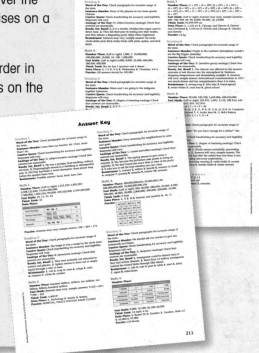

A Close-Up Look at the Practice Pages

Each of the double-sided reading practice pages includes the following skill-building features.

Reading (Side A)

> **Word of the Day** The first feature builds vocabulary by presenting a word and its definition. A brief writing task asks your child to use the new word to demonstrate understanding of its proper usage.

Reading 10 Side A

WORD of the Day

Use the word below in a short paragraph about a club or committee meeting.

agenda: (n.) *list of items of business for a meeting; a plan of things to be done or considered*

_____
_____
_____

> **Sentence Mender** This feature addresses conventions of Standard English, especially spelling, capitalization, punctuation, and grammar. Your child needs to rewrite a sentence with errors correctly. A sample answer is given in the Answer Key, but your child may devise alternative corrections.

Sentence Mender

Rewrite the sentence to make it correct.
Kelly look close at the foto Henry took.

_____

> **Cursive Quote** This section offers your child a chance to practice cursive handwriting as he or she copies and thinks about a quotation. Your child then writes a response to a question based on the quote. For this task, direct your child to use another sheet of paper.

Cursive Quote

Copy the quotation in cursive writing.
When it is dark enough, you can see the stars.
—Charles A. Beard

_____
_____

What do you think that Beard, a historian, meant by this? Write your answer in cursive on another sheet of paper.

> **Analogy of the Day** Every Side A concludes with an analogy that has one missing term. Your child determines the relationship between the first two words, then chooses a word to create a second pair of words that relate in the same way. He or she also writes a description of the relationship. These activities present a range of at least a dozen different types of analogies.

Analogy of the Day

Complete the analogy.

Ambiguous is to **obvious** as _____ is to
○ A. clear   ○ B. near   ○ C. distant   ○ D. away
Explain how the analogy works: _____
_____

Reading & Math Practice, Grade 6 © 2014 Scholastic Inc.

Reading (Side B)

Reading 10 Side B

📖 Ready, Set, READ!

Read the passage. Then answer the questions.

Visitors to the magnificent Grand Canyon can get an added treat with each trip. They can see the work of architect Mary Colter (1869–1958). She designed five impressive buildings along its South rim, like Hopi House, shown here.

Colter's work features bold, large-scale elements. One example is the amazing fireplace in her Bright Angel Lodge. Its rocks are arranged from floor to ceiling in the same geological order as they appear in the canyon walls! She built only with on-site materials. She used local Native American motifs in her buildings.

Colter completed 21 projects for Fred Harvey. His company operated the hotels and restaurants for the Santa Fe Railroad. When people got off the train to see the wonders of the West, they stayed in hotels Colter designed. She considered La Posada Hotel in Winslow, Arizona, her masterpiece. She designed just about everything for it, from its furniture to the maids' uniforms.

Mary Colter was among the few female architects of her time. She was among the very few who worked in such rugged conditions. Her work served as a model for structures built later by the National Park Service.

1. What role did Fred Harvey play in Colter's career?

_____

_____

2. What made Mary Colter unique? _____

_____

◑ BrainTeaser ◐

Unscramble each tree name.
Write it correctly in the spaces.
Then unscramble the boxed letters
to name something related to trees.

_____

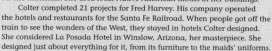

IRF	☐ __ __ __
CHOYIRK	__ __ __ __ __ ☐ __
RACED	__ ☐ __ __ __
LAWNTU	__ __ __ __ ☐ __
OHMCEKL	__ __ __ __ ☐ __ __
PANES	__ ☐ __ __ __

Math (Side A)

Number Place The first feature on Side A reviews place-value skills related to whole numbers, decimals, fractions, and integers. A solid place-value foundation is essential for success with computation and estimation, and for an overall grasp of numerical patterns and relationships.

Math **4**
Side A

Number Place

Complete the table.

Number	Millions	Thousands	Hundreds
1,700,000	1.7	1,700	17,000
8,000,000			80,000
1,800,000,000			
25,000,000,000		25,000,000	
34,500,000			

Fast Math

Estimate the sum by rounding to the greatest place of the least number.

1,825	5,226	29,341	1
3,079	468	8,254	60
+ 4,255	+ 8,375	+ 473	+ 5

Fast Math This activity addresses computation skills with the goal of building automaticity, fluency, and accuracy.

💡 Think Tank

Henry rode his bike 5 miles in 25 minutes. What was his average speed in miles per hour?

_____

At that rate, how far does Henry ride in half an hour?

_____

Show your work in the tank.

Think Tank This feature offers a word problem that draws from a wide spectrum of grade-appropriate skills, strategies, and approaches. In the think tank itself, your child can draw, do computations, and work out his or her thinking.

25

Reading & Math Practice, Grade 6 © 2014 Scholastic Inc.

Math (Side B)

> **Data Place** In this section, your child solves problems based on reading, collecting, representing, and interpreting data that is presented in many formats: lists, tables, charts, pictures, and, especially, graphs.

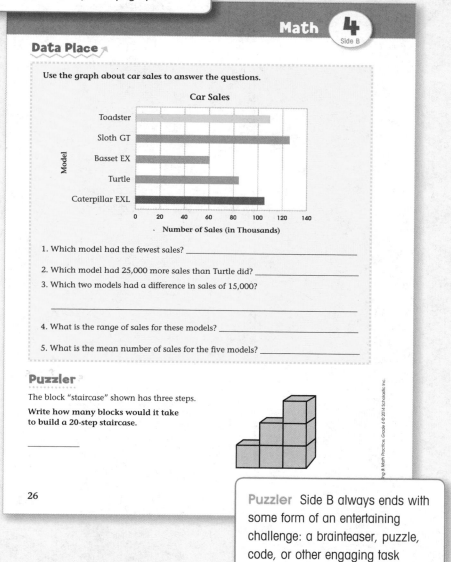

Math 4
Side B

Data Place

Use the graph about car sales to answer the questions.

Car Sales

(bar graph showing Number of Sales (in Thousands) for each Model)

Toadster, Sloth GT, Basset EX, Turtle, Caterpillar EXL

Number of Sales (in Thousands): 0 20 40 60 80 100 120 140

1. Which model had the fewest sales? _____

2. Which model had 25,000 more sales than Turtle did? _____

3. Which two models had a difference in sales of 15,000?

_____

4. What is the range of sales for these models? _____

5. What is the mean number of sales for the five models? _____

Puzzler

The block "staircase" shown has three steps.

Write how many blocks would it take to build a 20-step staircase.

_____

26

> **Puzzler** Side B always ends with some form of an entertaining challenge: a brainteaser, puzzle, code, or other engaging task designed to stretch the mind.

WORD of the Day

Use the word below in a short paragraph about a sporting event or a debate.

barrage: (n.) *a large number of words, blows, and so on, coming rapidly, one after the other*

_____

_____

_____

Sentence Mender

Rewrite the sentence to make it correct.

Luisa likes our teacher mr. Chen more than me do.

_____

Cursive Quote

Copy the quotation in cursive writing.

He who hates, hates himself.

—South African proverb

_____

_____

_____

Do you think the proverb makes sense? Explain. Write your answer in cursive on another sheet of paper.

Analogy of the Day

Complete the analogy.

Car is to **parking lot** as _____ is to **wallet**.

○ A. travel   ○ B. pocket   ○ C. leather   ○ D. money

Explain how the analogy works: _____

_____

Ready, Set, READ!

Read the story. Then answer the questions.

We had a small cottage just off the property of the hotel. My brother and I spent our summers there with Grandma. And every summer we saw at the hotel an elderly fellow known to us as Old Pete. From our house I could see him sitting, smoking his pipe, and rocking slowly on the porch of the dilapidated old Victorian that served the hotel as an annex. Staff slept there. And so, apparently, did Old Pete. I think the hotel fed him, too.

Old Pete wore the same dirty checkered red-and-black woolen coat every day no matter what the weather was. Most days he sat rocking all by himself. But upon occasion he'd come by to have coffee with Grandma. He rarely spoke, but I always knew he was there by the distinctive smells of wet wool and tobacco that went wherever he did. If he happened by while my brother and I were playing checkers, he'd come watch for a moment. Sometimes he mumbled something, usually of a disapproving nature. Grandma said Old Pete was related to us. My uncles disparagingly referred to him as the "old geezer" or "old fool."

But this summer there was no Old Pete. I asked Grandma about him. She smiled sadly. Indicating with her hand for me to follow, she walked to her desk. "He passed this winter. This obituary was in the paper," she said, handing it to me.

I read it aloud. It began: *Russian chess champion Sol Schwartz passed away at age 94. Schwartz, who ruled the chess world for two decades, died . . .*

1. How would you describe Old Pete?

_____

_____

_____

_____

2. Based on the passage what do think *disparagingly* means?

_____

_____

_____

_____

3. What was surprising about the obituary?

_____

_____

_____

_____

_____

◉ BrainTeaser ◉

Climb the word ladder to change *heat* to *fire*. Change only one letter at a time. Write the new word on each rung.

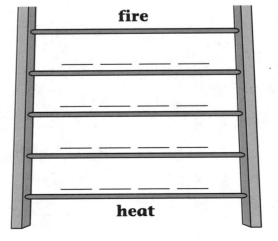

fire

heat

Reading & Math Practice, Grade 6 © 2014 Scholastic Inc.

Number Place

Write the number that is 1,000,000 *more.*

352,350 __1,325,350__   5,802,387 _____

2,307,122,050 _____   19,662,000,000 _____

Write the number that is 1,000,000 *less.*

8,500,000 _____   1,005,555,799,000 _____

500,020,000 _____   7,000,500,000 _____

Fast Math

Compute. Use the properties of addition and multiplication to help you find shortcuts.

$5 + 3^2 + 0 + 5 =$ _____

$1 \times 6^1 + 5 + 0 =$ _____

$3 \times (9 + 7 + 1) =$ _____

$2^1 + 0 + (4 \times 8) + 8 =$ _____

Think Tank

Ellie is numbering her 150-page scrapbook. How many times will she write the digit 4?

_____

Show your work in the tank.

Data Place

The table below shows results of a survey on favorite music groups. But some of the table is blank.

Use the clues to help you fill in the table.

• Twelve students chose Loud Enough.

• The Bugs got the most votes.

• Half as many who voted for Squash voted for Bunny and Hare.

• Fifty-six people took the survey

Music Group	Tally	Number
		8
		20

Puzzler

Use each digit from 1–9 to form three addends whose sum is 999.

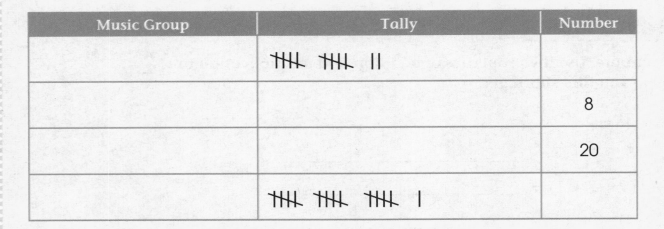

```
    ☐ ☐ ☐
    ☐ ☐ ☐
+   ☐ ☐ ☐
-----------
    9 9 9
```

WORD of the Day

Use the word below in a short paragraph about something you detest.

abominable: (adj.) *causing disgust, horror, or hatred; detestable*

_____

_____

_____

Sentence Mender

Rewrite the sentence to make it correct.

She hoping to be winning a metal in the track meat.

_____

Cursive Quote

Copy the quotation in cursive writing.

Fail to prepare, prepare to fail.

—Roy Keane

_____

_ _

_____

What did the writer mean? Explain. Write your answer in cursive on another sheet of paper.

Analogy of the Day

Complete the analogy.

Huge is to **enormous** as _____ is to **flat**.

○ A. bumpy   ○ B. level   ○ C. large   ○ D. pancake

Explain how the analogy works: _____

_____

Reading & Math Practice, Grade 6 © 2014 Scholastic Inc.

📖 Ready, Set, READ!

Read the passage. Then answer the questions.

A funny thing happened about 2,000 years ago in the Greek port of Alexandria, in Egypt. A priest lit an altar fire outside the doors of a temple. The fire heated water within a metal globe. The sealed globe was connected by a tube to a large bucket suspended by chains from a system of weights and pulleys. As the water expanded, it spilled through the tube into the bucket. As the bucket got heavier it pulled a rope that turned the temple doors on their pivots. The doors opened, as if by magic, just as people were arriving to worship. The priest may have used the world's first automatic door-opener.

Another funny thing happened when the priest left the temple. After he extinguished the fire, the air in the sphere cooled and contracted. This force siphoned the water from the bucket back into the sphere. The pulley system was activated in reverse. The bucket lightened and lifted. The temple doors closed.

This invention was attributed to Hero, a Greek mathematician and engineer. Hero liked to wow people with his "high tech" mechanical wonders. Historians cannot be certain that this device was actually built, though they have found written plans.

The next time your arms are loaded with packages and doors open to let you through, think of Hero tinkering away in his shop.

1. Why might worshipers have thought that the temple doors opened by magic?

_____

_____

2. What does it mean to *siphon* water? _____

_____

🌀 BrainTeaser 🌀

Use the clues to complete a word that starts with *cri*.

1. baby's bed   CRI ____

2. brittle   CRI ____ ____

3. disaster   CRI ____ ____ ____

4. cower   CRI ____ ____ ____

5. reviewers   CRI ____ ____ ____ ____

6. shade of red   CRI ____ ____ ____ ____

7. type of insect   CRI ____ ____ ____ ____

8. scrunches   CRI ____ ____ ____ ____ ____

Reading & Math Practice, Grade 6 © 2014 Scholastic Inc.

Number Place

Write the place of the underlined digit.

20,958,007,000 _____

362,004,185 _____

300,264,000,002 _____

15,000,040,312 _____

8,053,039,501,000 _____

74,068,289,040 _____

Fast Math

Use all the digits in the number bank each time to solve the riddles.

Number Bank

2 9 4 3 6 7 5

The sum of these two numbers is 10,089. What are the numbers?	The difference between these two numbers is 7,533. What are the numbers?

Think Tank

What is the area of the community garden?

_____

Show your work in the tank.

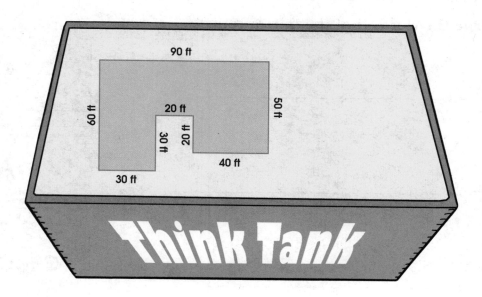

Data Place

The table shows average daily high temperatures in degrees Fahrenheit for some U.S. cities.

Use the data to answer the questions.

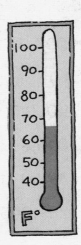

City	January	July
Anchorage, AK	22°	65°
Phoenix, AZ	65°	104°
Boston, MA	37°	82°
Seattle, WA	46°	75°

1. Which city's high winter temperature is about one-third of Phoenix's high winter temperature? _____

2. It is the middle of July and the temperature is 10° higher than it is on a typical day in Anchorage. Which city are you likely in? _____

3. Which city has the greatest difference between its January and July high temperatures? _____

Puzzler

The signs are how they look from the rearview mirror of a car.

Write the words that the mirror reflects.

_____

_____

_____

Reading & Math Practice, Grade 6 © 2014 Scholastic Inc.

WORD of the Day

Use the word below in a short paragraph about how someone or something annoys you.

irk: (v.) *to annoy or trouble*

_____

_____

_____

Sentence Mender

Rewrite the sentence to make it correct.

every morning the Neighborhood be calm, and quite.

_____

Cursive Quote

Copy the quotation in cursive writing.

Good fences make good neighbors.

—Robert Frost

_____

_____

_____

Do you agree? Explain. Write your answer in cursive on another sheet of paper.

Analogy of the Day

Complete the analogy.

Exhausted is to **sleep** as _____ is to **frown**.

○ A. happy   ○ B. tired   ○ C. sad   ○ D. awakened

Explain how the analogy works: _____

_____

📖 Ready, Set, READ!

Read the invitation. Then answer the questions.

COME TO A SURPRISE POOL PARTY!

Jeb is turning 12. Let's help him celebrate in style!
But please don't let the cat out of the bag. Jeb suspects *nothing*, since his actual birthday isn't until Monday.

Where: 23 Gracie Lane (corner of Robinson Street)

When: Saturday

What to bring: a smile, an appetite, a bathing suit, and a towel

What to wear: casual clothes and flip-flops

R.S.V.P. 555-5555

1. What does it mean to *let the cat out of the bag*? _____

_____

2. Will there be food there? How do you know? _____

_____

3. What information is missing from the invitation? _____

_____

4. R.S.V.P. are initials of French words. What do you think R.S.V.P. asks you to do?

_____

_____

⊚ BrainTeaser ⊚

Each word below starts and ends with the same letter.
But every missing letter pair is different. Complete the words.

1. ____ umm ____

2. ____ illo ____

3. ____ eart ____

4. ____ erami ____

5. ____ hrif ____

6. ____ regan ____

7. ____ arsni ____

8. ____ arach ____

9. ____ otato ____

10. ____ rmad ____

Reading & Math Practice, Grade 6 © 2014 Scholastic Inc.

Number Place

Write each number in standard form.

three hundred billion ten _____

fifty-nine billion one hundred thirty _____

six hundred six billion _____

thirty-two trillion one hundred four _____

Fast Math

Use mental math to find each product.

$4 \times 90 =$ _____ $\qquad$ $50 \times 600 =$ _____ $\qquad$ $7 \times 40{,}000 =$ _____

$7 \times 7{,}000 =$ _____ $\qquad$ $10^2 \times 80 =$ _____ $\qquad$ $10^2 \times 9{,}000 =$ _____

$60 \times 800 =$ _____ $\qquad$ $30 \times 10^3 =$ _____ $\qquad$ $70 \times 40{,}000 =$ _____

$500 \times 10^3 =$ _____ $\qquad$ $50 \times 10^4 =$ _____ $\qquad$ $10^1 \times 10^3 =$ _____

Think Tank

Ruth looks at a barnyard picture showing pigs, cows, and hens. She counts 17 heads and 56 legs. How many hens are in the picture?

_____

Show your work in the tank.

Data Place

Sixth grade students were asked to name their favorite kinds of books. The circle graph shows the results.

Use the data to answer the questions.

1. What fraction of the students chose fantasy?

_____

2. What fraction chose neither sports nor mystery?

_____

3. Which two kinds of books together got $\frac{3}{4}$ of the votes?

_____

4. There are 56 students in the 6th grade. What if 10 fewer voted for mystery and chose biography instead? How many votes would mystery then get in all? _____

   How many votes for biography? _____

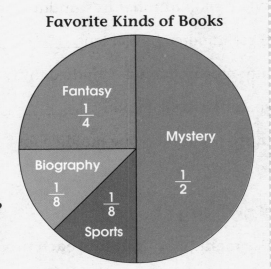

Favorite Kinds of Books

Fantasy $\frac{1}{4}$

Mystery $\frac{1}{2}$

Biography $\frac{1}{8}$

$\frac{1}{8}$ Sports

Puzzler

In the magic square, the sum of the numbers in each row, column, and diagonal is the same. This magic sum is the year the first person landed on the moon!

Complete the magic square.

387		383		408
393	405		397	
399	382	395	407	
409		396		392
381		406	390	

WORD of the Day

Use the word below in a short paragraph about courage in the face of a challenge.

grit: (n.) *courage in the face of danger or hardship; pluck*

_____

_____

_____

Sentence Mender

Rewrite the sentence to make it correct.

Us should ask are Teacher to give fewer homework on friday's.

_____

Cursive Quote

Copy the quotation in cursive writing.

Patience is bitter but its fruit is sweet.

—Anonymous

_____

_____

_____

What does this mean? Is it good advice? Explain. Write your answer in cursive on another sheet of paper.

Analogy of the Day

Complete the analogy.

Chew is to **swallow** as _____ is to **drink**.

○ A. pour   ○ B. napkin   ○ C. glass   ○ D. lemonade

Explain how the analogy works: _____

_____

📖 Ready, Set, READ!

Read the passage. Then answer the questions.

On January 2, 1892, Annie Moore was examined by doctors in the Great Hall. Annie was an Irish girl traveling with her two brothers. She was the first of more than 12 million people to enter the United States by way of Ellis Island.

The island is small and flat and lies in the shadow of the Statue of Liberty in New York harbor. It has had different uses over time. Once it was a prime spot for Native Americans to fish for oysters. It was once a safe place for pirates to hide. And it once served as a fort and as an ammunition dump. But from 1892 to 1954 it served its most important purpose. It was where immigrants were brought when their ships deposited them in the New York harbor. It was where they were processed and checked for signs of disease. Nearly all were allowed into the country. Only about two out of every 100 were not.

Ellis Island is now part of the Statue of Liberty National Monument. It now looks like it did a century ago. More than two million people visit every year. They don't need to get medical exams. But they do get to see an important piece of American history.

1. Why were some immigrants denied entry? _____

_____

2. Why is Ellis Island an important place? _____

_____

🌀 BrainTeaser 🌀

An *anagram* is a new word made using all the letters of another word. *Tap* is an anagram for *pat*.

Make an anagram for each word.

1. dire ⇔ _____

2. veto ⇔ _____

3. tape ⇔ _____

4. bleat ⇔ _____

5. tarts ⇔ _____

6. diary ⇔ _____

7. eager ⇔ _____

8. smile ⇔ _____

Reading & Math Practice, Grade 6 © 2014 Scholastic Inc.

Number Place

Complete the table.

Number	Millions	Thousands	Hundreds
1,700,000	1.7	1,700	17,000
8,000,000			80,000
1,800,000,000			
25,000,000,000		25,000,000	
34,500,000			

Fast Math

Estimate the sum by rounding to the greatest place of the least number.

$$
\begin{array}{r}
1,825 \\
3,079 \\
+\ 4,255 \\
\hline
\end{array}
\qquad
\begin{array}{r}
5,226 \\
468 \\
+\ 8,375 \\
\hline
\end{array}
\qquad
\begin{array}{r}
29,341 \\
8,254 \\
+\quad 473 \\
\hline
\end{array}
\qquad
\begin{array}{r}
1,574 \\
60,327 \\
+\ 5,552 \\
\hline
\end{array}
$$

Think Tank

Henry rode his bike 5 miles in 25 minutes. What was his average speed in miles per hour?

_____

At that rate, how far does Henry ride in half an hour?

_____

Show your work in the tank.

Reading & Math Practice, Grade 6 © 2014 Scholastic Inc.

Data Place

Use the graph about car sales to answer the questions.

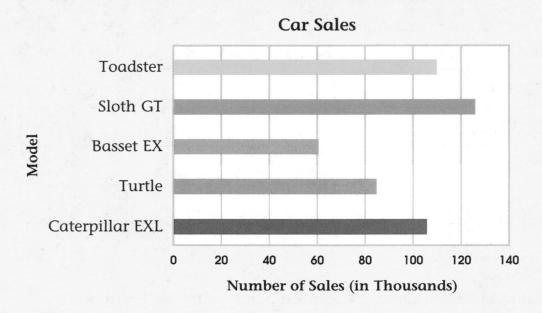

Car Sales

Model / Number of Sales (in Thousands)

1. Which model had the fewest sales? _____

2. Which model had 25,000 more sales than Turtle did? _____

3. Which two models had a difference in sales of 15,000?

    _____

4. What is the range of sales for these models? _____

5. What is the mean number of sales for the five models? _____

Puzzler

The block "staircase" shown has three steps.

**Write how many blocks would it take
to build a 20-step staircase.**

_____

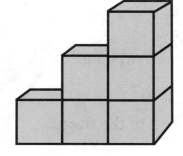

26

Reading & Math Practice, Grade 6 © 2014 Scholastic Inc.

WORD of the Day

Use the word below in a short descriptive paragraph about how bad weather affected a planned event.

adverse: (adj.) *unfriendly in purpose or effect; antagonistic; hostile*

_____

_____

_____

Sentence Mender

Rewrite the sentence to make it correct.

Nun of the players on we're Team speaks chinese.

_____

Cursive Quote

Copy the quotation in cursive writing.

The teeth are smiling, but is the heart?

—African proverb

- -

- -

- -

What is the meaning of this proverb? Write your answer in cursive on another sheet of paper.

Analogy of the Day

Complete the analogy.

Sandwich is to **lunch box** as _____ is to **closet**.

○ A. couch　　○ B. breakfast　　○ C. house　　○ D. coat

Explain how the analogy works: _____

_____

Ready, Set, READ!

Read the passage. Then answer the questions.

Many marine biologists agree that the hagfish might be the world's most disgusting fish. Whether it is or is not, it is surely a very unusual sea creature. For starters, is it even a fish? There is some debate because this long, wormlike creature is way more primitive than most fish and may in fact be more closely related to eel-like creatures called lampreys.

The hagfish is usually no longer than a yard in length. It has no true fins and is the only living animal with a skull but no vertebral column. It has a jawless round mouth and several slender, whisker-like organs surrounding it. These barbels are like those that catfish have. They serve as taste buds. The hagfish dives into its food. Literally. It feeds on other fish by boring into their bodies. And that's not the really disgusting part.

What's truly revolting is what the hagfish does when caught or otherwise agitated. It releases an ample amount of thick, slimy mucus. Then it cleans itself of the gooey slime by tying itself into an overhand knot, scraping it off as it does so. The other sea creatures have no such ability.

1. What is a *barbel*? _____

_____

2. Why do many scientists think the hagfish is disgusting?

_____

_____

◉ BrainTeaser ◉

Begin with a number word and use all 14 words in the word bank once to make a tongue twister. Write your idea below. Then try to say it three times in a row fast!

Word Bank

and	bricks
chicks	kicky
picks	six
sixty	slick
spikes	sticky
sticks	strike
thick	with

_____

_____

Reading & Math Practice, Grade 6 © 2014 Scholastic Inc.

Number Place

Write each power of 10 in standard form.

$10^3 =$ _____ $10^0 =$ _____

$10^7 =$ _____ $10^8 =$ _____

$10^4 =$ _____ $10^1 =$ _____

$10^2 =$ _____ $10^6 =$ _____

Fast Math →

Estimate by rounding each factor to its greatest place.

$31 \times 209 =$ _____ $7 \times 768 =$ _____

$46 \times 542 =$ _____ $84 \times 6{,}441 =$ _____

$57 \times 3{,}299 =$ _____ $610 \times 980 =$ _____

Think Tank

Mike asks Ike for change for a dollar. Ike tells Mike that although he has $1.15 in change, he cannot make change for a dollar. Mike tells Ike that he certainly can. Who is right? Explain.

_____

_____

_____

_____

Show your work in the tank.

Data Place

Leah and her brother Ray compared the amount of time each spent on homework one week. The graph shows the results.

Use the data to answer the questions.

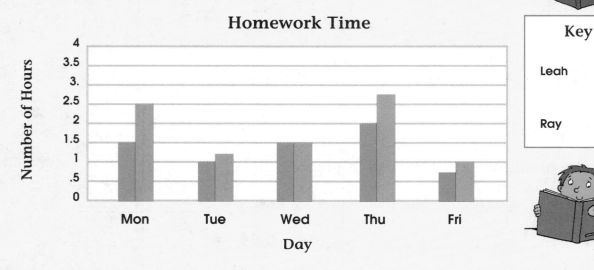

1. How much longer than Leah did Ray work on Monday? _____

2. How much less did Leah work on Friday than she did on Wednesday? _____

3. On which day did the two work for the same amount of time? _____

4. On which day did they work the longest? _____

   How long altogether did they work that day? _____

Puzzler

Try this number trick. Start with *any* five-digit number. But make sure that the difference between the first and last digits is at least 2.

Write your number here _____

• Swap the first and last digits.
• Subtract the smaller number from the larger one.
• Swap the first and last digits.
• Add these two numbers. What is the sum? _____
• Now try the trick with other 5-digit numbers. What do you notice?

Reading & Math Practice, Grade 6 © 2014 Scholastic Inc.

WORD of the Day

Use the word below in a short paragraph about a wild animal on the hunt.

prowl: (v.) *go about secretly and slowly in search of something to eat or steal*

_____

_____

_____

Sentence Mender

Rewrite the sentence to make it correct.

Brian and me is going to the Ballgame together to morrow.

_____

Cursive Quote

Copy the quotation in cursive writing.

Energy and persistence conquer all things.

—Benjamin Franklin

- -

- -

- -

Is this good advice? Explain. Write your explanation in cursive on another sheet of paper.

Analogy of the Day

Complete the analogy.

Small is to **minuscule** as _____ is to **miserable**.

○ A. little   ○ B. sad   ○ C. wretched   ○ D. excited

Explain how the analogy works: _____

_____

Ready, Set, READ!

Read the passage. Then answer the questions.

An **isthmus** is a narrow strip of land bordered on both sides by water that connects two larger bodies of land. The term comes from the Greek word *isthmos*, a narrow neck of land. Its counterpart is a *strait*. A strait is a narrow channel of water that links two larger navigable bodies of water. The term *strait* commonly describes a navigable water passage between two land masses.

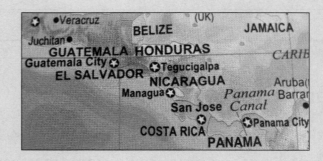

The shipping industry certainly knows the true meaning of isthmus. That's because many canals are built through them as time-saving shortcuts in shipping routes. The Panama Canal and Suez Canal are examples. The former is located on the Isthmus of Panama. It links the Caribbean Sea and Atlantic Ocean with the Pacific Ocean. The latter was built on the Isthmus of Suez. It connects the Red Sea with the Mediterranean Sea.

1. An isthmus is a
   - ○ A. canal.
   - ○ B. neck of land.
   - ○ C. water passage between two land masses.
   - ○ D. strip of land linking two larger land masses.

2. The Panama Canal connects which two bodies of water?
   - ○ A. Red Sea and Mediterranean Sea
   - ○ B. Caribbean Sea and Pacific Ocean
   - ○ C. Caribbean Sea and Atlantic Ocean
   - ○ D. Pacific Ocean and Red Sea

◎ BrainTeaser ◎

Onomatopoeia is a word that sounds like what it means. Examples are *buzz*, *hiss*, and *oink*.

Finish each simple sentence using onomatopoeia.

1. Springs _____ .

2. Knights in armor _____ .

3. Autumn leaves _____ .

4. Sleigh bells _____ .

5. Wheat fields _____ .

6. Mud _____ .

Reading & Math Practice, Grade 6 © 2014 Scholastic Inc.

Number Place

Write each as a power of 10.

100 = _____   1 = _____

10,000 = _____   1,000,000 = _____

1,000 = _____   10,000,000 = _____

Fast Math →

Find the value of y. Use basic facts to help you.

$240 \div 3 = y$ _____ $280 \div 7 = y$ _____ $4,800 \div 6 = y$ _____

$y = 810 \div 9$ _____ $y = 600 \div 5$ _____ $y = 2,000 \div 40$ _____

Compare. Write <, =, or >.

$36,000 \div 6$ _____ $40,000 \div 8$ $450,000 \div 90$ _____ $2,500 \div 50$

Think Tank

The team orders 4 tacos, a foot-long dog, 2 burgers, 3 sliders, and two of each kind of drink. Coach buys a drink for himself and pays for all with a $100 bill. His change is $28.14. Which drink did he order?

_____

Show your work in the tank.

TAKE-OUT MENU	
Foot-long Dog .. $9.95	Juice $2.59
Burger $7.79	Soda $1.75
Taco . . . . $4.95 each	Milk . , ... $1.50
Pork Slider. . . . . . . $3.95 each	Tea. $1.00

Think Tank

Data Place

Use the calendar to answer the questions.

What are the dates?

1. Five in a row have a mean of 21. _____

2. Three in a row have a product of 1,716. _____

3. Two in a row have a product of 812 and a sum of 57. _____

4. Two are prime numbers with a product of 493. _____

5. Three consecutive odd dates have a product of 4,845. _____

_____

APRIL

SUN	MON	TUE	WED	THU	FRI	SAT
			1	2	3	4
5	6	7	8	9	10	11
12	13	14	15	16	17	18
19	20	21	22	23	24	25
26	27	28	29	30		

Puzzler

Look at the numbers in the number bank. What do they all have in common?

_____

_____

_____

Number Bank

15   62   37

26   48

51   84   73

95   59

WORD of the Day

Use the word below in a short paragraph about a crime.

culprit: (n.) *a person guilty of misconduct or a crime; an offender*

_____

_____

_____

Sentence Mender

Rewrite the sentence to make it correct.

The eiffel tower is the taller strukture in paris france.

_____

Cursive Quote

Copy the quotation in cursive writing.

The time is always right to do what is right.

—Dr. Martin Luther King, Jr.

Do you agree? Write your answer in cursive on another sheet of paper.

Analogy of the Day

Complete the analogy.

Finger is to **hand** as _____ is to **tree**.

○ A. forest   ○ B. branch   ○ C. toe   ○ D. maple

Explain how the analogy works: _____

_____

📖 Ready, Set, READ!

Read the following letter that appeared in a local newspaper. Then answer the questions.

Have you been in any of our town parks lately? If so, you must have noticed that they need our help. The trash cans are overflowing. The grass is too long. Weeds grow wherever they please. Playground equipment needs repair and cleaning. Snow removal on paths doesn't happen soon enough. Many of the lamps need bulbs. I could go on and on. I know that our parks are in crisis. I know, too, that our town is short of money and workers.

Help can be on the way: our help. We upper-elementary and middle-school students can step up to the plate and do some good. I ask for volunteers from every class to join me in fixing our wonderful parks. I've spoken with people in the mayor's office. They are behind the idea. They promise to supply us with whatever tools and guidance we need. They promise to identify the most urgent problems. They say they will teach us what we need to know. I have their support. I just need you.

So, join me, won't you? Put in just a few hours of park work each week. You'll make our parks look great again. And you'll feel great, too!

1. What is the central message of this letter? _____

_____

2. What first step did the writer take to get this project going? _____

_____

3. How would you describe the tone of this letter? _____

_____

🌀 BrainTeaser 🌀

A *palindrome* is a word that reads the same forward and backward.

Write a palindrome for each clue.

1. long heroic stories _____

2. female sheep _____

3. related to citizenship _____

4. girl's name _____

5. hang new wall covering _____

Reading & Math Practice, Grade 6 © 2014 Scholastic Inc.

Number Place

Write each number in expanded form using exponents.

1,005 _____

216 _____

42,906 _____

840,000 _____

2,075,000 _____

3,660,000,000 _____

Fast Math

Use compatible numbers to estimate each quotient.

2,157 ÷ 5 = _____   4,851 ÷ 7 = _____   80,026 ÷ 90 = _____

3,579 ÷ 68 = _____   5,513 ÷ 66 = _____   630,792 ÷ 79 = _____

621,004 ÷ 7 = _____   3,507 ÷ 313 = _____   395,122 ÷ 42 = _____

Think Tank

Rounded to the nearest million, the average distance from the earth to the sun is about 93,000,000 miles. What is the greatest whole number the actual distance could be?

_____

Show your work in the tank.

Data Place

The table shows distances between some cities on Thin Airlines.

Use the data to answer the questions.

Airline Mileage (one way)

City	Chicago	Cleveland	Denver	Detroit	Omaha
Chicago		308	920	238	432
Cleveland	308		1,227	90	739
Denver	920	1,227		1,156	488
Detroit	238	90	1,156		669
Omaha	432	739	488	669	

1. How far is it from Denver to Detroit? _____

2. Which two cities are 920 miles apart? _____

3. Which two cities are farthest apart? _____

4. How many miles is the roundtrip from Cleveland to Omaha? _____

5. Captain Flyte made two roundtrips between two cities for a total distance of 952 miles. Between which two cities did he fly? _____

6. Flight attendant Bev Ridge made three roundtrips between two cities in which she logged 2,928 miles. Between which two cities did she fly?

_____

Puzzler

A cabinet filled with clothing weighs 27 kg. The same cabinet filled with books weighs 132 kg. If the books weigh 8 times what the clothing weighs, how much does the cabinet weigh?

_____

WORD of the Day

Use the word below in a short paragraph about a healthy diet.

wholesome: (adj.) *good for the health; healthy*

_____

_____

_____

Sentence Mender

Rewrite the sentence to make it correct.

poeple in the northern himsphere could'nt see the big dipper yesterday.

_____

Cursive Quote

Copy the quotation in cursive writing.

Painting is just another way of keeping a diary.

—Pablo Picasso

_____

_____

_____

What do you think Picasso meant by this? Write your answer in cursive on another sheet of paper.

Analogy of the Day

Complete the analogy.

Student is to **class** as _____ is to **team**.

○ A. coach   ○ B. league   ○ C. teacher   ○ D. athlete

Explain how the analogy works: _____

_____

📖 Ready, Set, READ!

Read the passage. Then answer the questions.

Krakatoa erupted off the coast of Java in 1883. Nearly 40,000 people died in the huge tsunami that followed this famous volcanic eruption. The effects of the immense waves were felt as far away as France. Dust swirled in the atmosphere, causing temperatures to plummet. The eruption was a monstrous event. Telegraph wires buzzed with the bad news. But was this the most devastating eruption ever?

It was not. That "honor" belongs to Indonesia's Mt. Tambora, which blew in 1815. That 14,000-foot cone-shaped mountain exploded over a period of ten days. A crater four miles wide and 3,540 feet deep formed within the damaged mountain.

Dr. Haraldur Sigurdsson of the University of Rhode Island said of the Mt. Tambora eruption: "This is the volcano that has caused most destruction on earth, the greatest death toll of any eruption on the earth, the greatest climate impact on the earth." Ash in the air blocked sunlight in the area for several days. And then things got worse. The swirling cloud spread around the world. Temperatures dropped and crops failed across the northern hemisphere. In Europe, 1816 became known as "the year without a summer."

Tambora may not be the best known volcanic eruption. But it was surely the most terrible.

1. Why was 1816 called "the year without a summer?" _____

_____

2. What might explain the lack of knowledge about the Tambora eruption?

_____

_____

🌀 BrainTeaser 🌀

Hink Pinks are one-syllable word pairs that rhyme to fit clues.

Example

angry father = mad dad

Solve these Hink Pink riddles.

1. What is the incorrect melody? _____

2. What is an artificial body of water? _____

3. What is a condiment for toast? _____

4. What is a pig's complaint?_____

5. What is an angry supervisor? _____

6. What is an academy for ghosts? _____

Reading & Math Practice, Grade 6 © 2014 Scholastic Inc.

Number Place

Write each in standard form.

$(9 \times 10^4) + (6 \times 10^2)$ _____

$(3 \times 10^5) + (2 \times 10^4) + (7 \times 10^2)$ _____

$(5 \times 10^6) + (4 \times 10^5) + (9 \times 10^3) + (6 \times 10^0)$ _____

$(6 \times 10^8) + (1 \times 10^4) + (8 \times 10^1)$ _____

Fast Math

Find each quotient and remainder.

$5,777 \div 34 =$ _____ $72,072 \div 72 =$ _____ $400,458 \div 186 =$ _____

$1,634 \div 15 =$ _____ $36,389 \div 82 =$ _____ $88,408 \div 514 =$ _____

$2,710 \div 759 =$ _____ $28,671 \div 57 =$ _____ $113,642 \div 364 =$ _____

Think Tank

Consecutive numbers are numbers in counting order. The sum of the squares of four consecutive numbers is 230. What is the sum of the numbers themselves?

_____

Show your work in the tank.

Data Place

Study the coordinate grid to see some places in Tim's town:

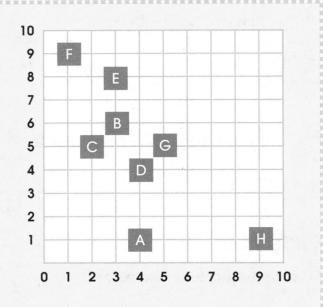

A Coffee Shop	**B** Fire Station
C Main Square	**D** Newsstand
E Audio Mart	**F** Parking Garage
G Bob's Bakery	**H** Computer City

Name the ordered pair for each point.

1. **A** _____   2. **F** _____   3. **H** _____   4. **C** _____

Name the point and the place it represents.

5. (9, 1) _____

6. (4, 4) _____

7. (3, 8) _____

8. (5, 5) _____

Puzzler

Each letter represents a digit.

Find the missing digits in the problem.

$$\begin{array}{r} A\,B\,C\,D \\ \times \quad\quad 4 \\ \hline D\,C\,B\,A \end{array}$$

A = _____   B = _____   C = _____   D = _____

Reading & Math Practice, Grade 6 © 2014 Scholastic Inc.

WORD of the Day

Use the word below in a short paragraph about reactions to an unfair law or rule.

denounce: (v.) *condemn openly; express strong disapproval of*

_____

_____

_____

Sentence Mender

Rewrite the sentence to make it correct.

"Dew you has change of a dollar, she ask".

_____

Cursive Quote

Copy the quotation in cursive writing.

If you would be loved, love, and be lovable.

—Benjamin Franklin

- -

Is this good advice? Explain. Write your answer in cursive on another sheet of paper.

Analogy of the Day

Complete the analogy.

Dirty is to **filthy** as _____ is to **exhilarated**.

○ A. clean   ○ B. ecstatic   ○ C. happy   ○ D. miserable

Explain how the analogy works: _____

_____

Ready, Set, READ!

Read the story. Then answer the questions.

If it weren't for a cluster of parked cars, we'd never have found the cave. Its entrance was mostly hidden. All we could see was a slit of darkness maybe 30 feet down a rocky slope. This was not going to be one of those safe, well-lit caves with handrails and cleared pathways. We turned on our flashlights, and warily clambered down.

The initial descent was rough. It took several minutes of climbing down jagged rocks before we found ourselves in total darkness. And I mean total. We couldn't see our hands without a flashlight. It was cold, too. We untied our flannel shirts from our waists and put them on. Then we began to explore.

The going got more level but never much easier. The cave opened up to the size of a subway tunnel. We walked cautiously, since many surfaces were sharp and others wet and slippery. We were scared, too. We feared falling or losing our way. And the thought of meeting up with any inhabitants of the cave was worrisome. We never did see another person the whole time we spent underground.

The journey back out was just as hazardous as the one going in. Carefully, we navigated our way, seeking the best route, struggling to keep our balance. Eventually we made it. We cheered and high-fived as we emerged into the light. What an awesome adventure! We had an amazing time—didn't we?

1. What do you think *warily* means?

_____

2. What do you think the writer means in the last sentence?

_____

☙ BrainTeaser ❧

Hinky Pinkies are two-syllable word pairs that rhyme to fit clues.
Solve these Hinky Pinky riddles.

Example

arctic tooth = polar molar

1. What is beautiful sprinting? _____

2. What is a war among steers? _____

3. Who is a crabby New York ballplayer? _____

4. Who steals cantaloupes? _____

5. What is the central violinist? _____

6. What is a finer cardigan? _____

Reading & Math Practice, Grade 6 © 2014 Scholastic Inc.

Number Place

Compare. Write <, =, or >.

788,000 _____ 780,000,000

606,666,000 _____ 606,000,666

87,000,000,000 _____ 970,000,000

fifty million _____ 50,000,000

four hundred four billion _____ 400,000,004

three trillion five hundred million _____ 3,500,000,000

Fast Math

Write the tenth number in each sequence.

0.4, 0.6, 0.8, 1.0, 1.2, 1.4, . . . _____

1.2, 4.2, 9.2, 16.2, 25.2, 36.2, . . . _____

0.1, 0.5, 0.3, 0.7, 0.5, 0.9, . . . _____

Think Tank

The total area of Taiwan is 13,892 square miles. Tajikistan is 41,359 square miles larger. Tanzania's total area is 364,900 square miles. How much smaller than Tanzania is Tajikistan?

_____

Show your work in the tank.

Reading & Math Practice, Grade 6 © 2014 Scholastic Inc.

Data Place

In each grid below, locate the points for the ordered pairs. Connect the points in order and then connect the last point to the first one. Then write *isosceles, equilateral,* or *scalene* to describe the triangle you have formed.

1. A (1, 1), B (3, 3), C (7, 1)

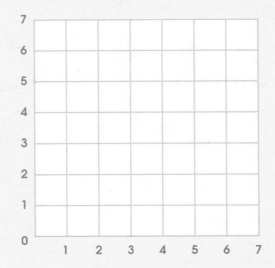

_____

2. D (3, 1), E (0, 7), F (6, 4)

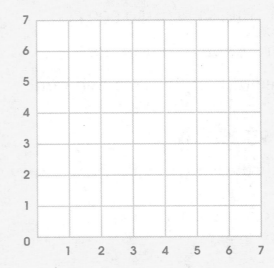

_____

Puzzler

Try this toothpick challenge: Remove 6 toothpicks to form two triangles.

Show your answer.

Reading & Math Practice, Grade 6 © 2014 Scholastic Inc.

WORD of the Day

Use the word below in a short paragraph about a club or committee meeting.

agenda: (n.) *list of items of business for a meeting; a plan of things to be done or considered*

_____

_____

_____

Sentence Mender

Rewrite the sentence to make it correct.

Kelly look close at the foto Henry took.

_____

Cursive Quote

Copy the quotation in cursive writing.

When it is dark enough, you can see the stars.

—Charles A. Beard

- -

- -

- -

What do you think that Beard, a historian, meant by this? Write your answer in cursive on another sheet of paper.

Analogy of the Day

Complete the analogy.

Ambiguous is to **obvious** as _____ is to **far**.

○ A. clear   ○ B. near   ○ C. distant   ○ D. away

Explain how the analogy works: _____

_____

Ready, Set, READ!

Read the passage. Then answer the questions.

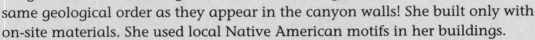

Visitors to the magnificent Grand Canyon can get an added treat with each trip. They can see the work of architect Mary Colter (1869–1958). She designed five impressive buildings along its South rim, like Hopi House, shown here.

Colter's work features bold, large-scale elements. One example is the amazing fireplace in her Bright Angel Lodge. Its rocks are arranged from floor to ceiling in the same geological order as they appear in the canyon walls! She built only with on-site materials. She used local Native American motifs in her buildings.

Colter completed 21 projects for Fred Harvey. His company operated the hotels and restaurants for the Santa Fe Railroad. When people got off the train to see the wonders of the West, they stayed in hotels Colter designed. She considered La Posada Hotel in Winslow, Arizona, her masterpiece. She designed just about everything for it, from its furniture to the maids' uniforms.

Mary Colter was among the few female architects of her time. She was among the very few who worked in such rugged conditions. Her work served as a model for structures built later by the National Park Service.

1. What role did Fred Harvey play in Colter's career?

_____

_____

2. What made Mary Colter unique? _____

_____

🌀 BrainTeaser 🌀

Unscramble each tree name.
Write it correctly in the spaces.
Then unscramble the boxed letters
to name something related to trees.

_____

IRF ☐ ___ ___

CHOYIRK ___ ___ ___ ___ ___ ☐ ___

RACED ___ ☐ ___ ___ ___

LAWNTU ___ ___ ___ ___ ☐ ___

OHMCEKL ___ ___ ___ ☐ ___ ___ ___

PANES ___ ☐ ___ ___ ___

Reading & Math Practice, Grade 6 © 2014 Scholastic Inc.

Number Place

Write the decimal.

eight tenths _____

six hundredths _____

sixty-three hundredths _____

sixteen thousandths _____

nine ten-thousandths _____

one and two hundredths _____

Fast Math

Find each sum or difference.

7 + 8.56 = _____

0.852 + 0.45 + 0.2613 = _____

2.08 + 0.707 = _____

9.3 + 0.4637 + 0.5441 = _____

8 – 2.0476 = _____

0.91 – 0.745 = _____

Think Tank

Rosie bought a painting for $1,000. She sold it for $1,200. Then she bought it back for $1,500 and sold it again for $1,800. In the end, did she make or lose money? How much?

_____

Show your work in the tank.

Data Place

The students in Ms. Bunsen's science class took a quiz today. The line plot shows their scores.

Use the data to answer the questions.

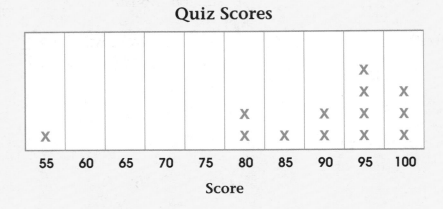

Quiz Scores

1. How many students took the quiz? _____

2. Which score is an outlier? _____

3. Around which score do the data cluster? _____

4. What are the range, mean, median, and mode of the scores?

   _____

5. What are the range, mean, median, and mode of the scores *without* the outlier?

   _____

Puzzler

1. What do the dates March 16, 1948, February 25, 1950, and August 8, 1964 have in common?

   _____

2. What were the *first* three dates in 2012 that have a similar pattern?

   _____

Reading & Math Practice, Grade 6 © 2014 Scholastic Inc.

WORD of the Day

Use the word below in a short paragraph about a sailboat or ship.

taut: (adj.) *tightly drawn; tense; in neat condition; tidy*

_____

_____

_____

Sentence Mender

Rewrite the sentence to make it correct.

Us visited the little big horn National battlefield in Suthern montana.

_____

Cursive Quote

Copy the quotation in cursive writing.

Women can do everything; men can do the rest.

—Russian proverb

_____

_____

_____

Do you agree with this proverb? Write your answer in cursive on another sheet of paper.

Analogy of the Day

Complete the analogy.

Lamp is to **light** as _____ is to **open**.

○ A. corkscrew   ○ B. twist   ○ C. bottle   ○ D. cork

Explain how the analogy works: _____

_____

📖 Ready, Set, READ!

Read the passage. Then answer the questions.

TWINS CLOBBER MARLINS . . . GIANTS SPLIT DOUBLE HEADER! PIRATES TAKE TWO FROM ROYALS, THEN BEAT ORIOLES . . .

Just imagine how these headlines would look to someone unfamiliar with our American pastime, baseball. *Clobbering a marlin? Beating an oriole?* Ouch!

Baseball has its own special language and idioms based on simple words. A close, tense game is a nail-biter. A game with lots of scoring is a slugfest. No runs are scored by a team that is shut out. In a rare perfect game, no player on the losing team ever gets on base.

Batters try to hit a pitched ball. If the ball crosses home plate within the strike zone, it is called a strike—even if the batter doesn't swing at it. If the ball misses the strike zone, it is called a ball. Most often, players who connect with the ball hit fouls, pop-ups, grounders, dribblers (little nubbers), and bunts. They try to hit the ball in the gaps, up the middle, or out of the park. Sometimes, batters simply ground out or fly out.

Pitchers stand on a rubber and look toward the plate for a sign from the catcher. They throw knucklers, sliders, split-finger fastballs, forkballs, even spitters. Once in a while they'll balk or get tossed by an umpire for beaning a batter. Ouch! Fielders trap grounders, get put-outs, make errors, and lose the ball in the sun. It's not an easy game.

1. What kind of hit might a player get?
   - ○ A. grounder
   - ○ B. rubber
   - ○ C. slider
   - ○ D. balk

2. A pitcher might get tossed out of a game for
   - ○ A. spitting.
   - ○ B. bunting.
   - ○ C. dribbling.
   - ○ D. hitting a batter.

3. What does *rare* mean?
   - ○ A. frequent
   - ○ B. real
   - ○ C. unusual
   - ○ D. losing

☼ BrainTeaser ☼

Write a synonym from the word bank for each boldface word below.

1. **forsake** them _____

2. had **misgivings** _____

3. **ingenious** plan _____

4. **adverse** conditions _____

5. shameless **hypocrite** _____

6. **maximum** speed _____

7. remarkable **stamina** _____

8. **mimic** the player _____

Word Bank

difficult
disown
endurance
parrot
phony
qualms
resourceful
utmost

Number Place

Write the value of the variable.

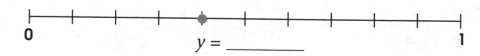

$y =$ _____

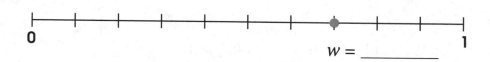

$w =$ _____

Fast Math

Estimate the product by rounding each factor to its greatest place.

$4.21 \times 2.3 =$	$6.56 \times 8.8 =$	$9.5 \times 0.85 =$	$83.405 \times 0.63 =$
_____	_____	_____	_____
$15.92 \times 0.96 =$	$9.645 \times 4.1 =$	$93.17 \times 0.92 =$	$15.805 \times 3.46 =$
_____	_____	_____	_____

Think Tank

A meter is approximately 39.37 inches long. To the nearest inch, how long is one meter?

_____

To the nearest foot, how long is one kilometer?

_____

Show your work in the tank.

Data Place

The table shows scoring in a football league.

The Bees played the Moths.

Use the clues to fill in the scoreboard.

Touchdown	6 points
Touchdown With Extra Point	7 points
Field Goal	3 points
Safety	2 points

• Each team scored a field goal in the first quarter.

• The Moths led by 1 point at the half.

• The Bees scored a touchdown with an extra point and a field goal in the third quarter. In the fourth quarter, they scored a touchdown and a safety.

• The Moths scored a safety in the third quarter and two touchdowns with extra points in the last quarter.

Quarter	1	2	3	4	Final Score
Bees		6			
Moths					

Puzzler

The bus route from Turtle to Dove is shown below. How many trips between stops are possible?

_____

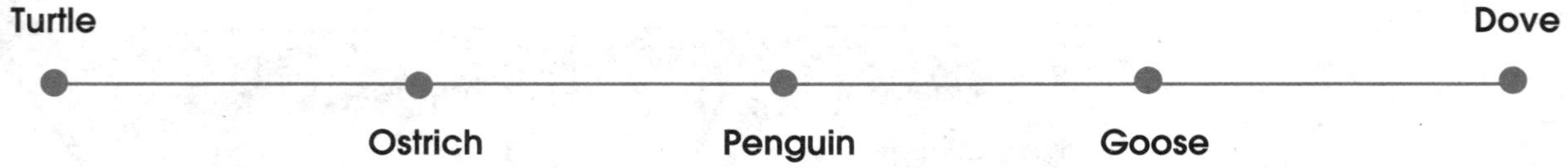

Turtle   Ostrich   Penguin   Goose   Dove

Reading & Math Practice, Grade 6 © 2014 Scholastic Inc.

WORD of the Day

Use the word below in a short paragraph about a politician running for office.

distort: (v.) *twist out of shape; give a false or misleading account of; misrepresent*

_____

_____

_____

Sentence Mender

Rewrite the sentence to make it correct.

In every Town you have your disagreemints over raisin taxis.

_____

Cursive Quote

Copy the quotation in cursive writing.

The man who has no imagination has no wings.

—Mohammed Ali

_____

_____

_____

What did Ali mean by this? Write your answer in cursive on another sheet of paper.

Analogy of the Day

Complete the analogy.

Linguine is to **pasta** as _____ is to **tree**.

○ A. oak   ○ B. leaf   ○ C. forest   ○ D. branch

Explain how the analogy works: _____

_____

Ready, Set, READ!

Read the passage. Then answer the questions.

People had long been taking rides on what were known as "pleasure wheels." They sat in chairs suspended from wooden rings turned by hand. Then, in 1893, the Ferris wheel arrived.

George Washington Ferris was an engineer. He built a reputation constructing sturdy bridges across the Ohio River. Ferris was asked to construct something special for the World Columbian Exposition in Chicago. He jumped at the chance. What he came up with was the highlight of the exposition.

Ferris's wheel was 264 feet tall and rotated on a 71-ton axle. It could carry 2,160 people high into the air and then back down. Up to 60 passengers rode in each of 36 cars; some sat, others stood. A 50¢ ride consisted of two revolutions that lasted a total of 20 minutes. The first revolution took longer because it made six stops at which terrified riders could get off.

The Ferris wheel is now the most common type of ride at state fairs. And it has spread around the world. In 2008, the Singapore Flyer opened for business. Soaring 541 feet into the air, it is currently the world's tallest Ferris wheel.

1. Why did George Ferris construct his wheel? _____

_____

2. In what way did the operators of the wheel account for riders' fears?

_____

_____

⟲ BrainTeaser ⟳

The word bank lists language arts words. Each word is hidden in the puzzle. Find and circle each word.

Word Bank

ADJECTIVE	NOUN	SENTENCE
ADVERB	PARAGRAPH	SINGULAR
ANTONYM	PERIOD	SUBJECT
CLAUSE	PHRASE	SYNONYM
COLON	PLURAL	TENSE
COMMA	PROPER	TOPIC
GRAMMAR	QUESTION	VERB
HYPHEN	REVISE	
MODIFY	ROOT	

```
W S N L Z H A A N P S X V N Y P W
G U Y D Y A D M A O S T E O T L R
G B E P F V N R M Y I X R L Y U A
N J H Y E Q A T F O J T B O V R L
W E W R D G A I O F C L S C E A U
N C B R R W D E C N E T N E S L G
D T O A D O J S X Y Y V Y R U I N
N O P R M R E P O R P M A P A Q I
T H I J E K C L O Q G M H J L I S
G K R R Q V T U S G M S N M C C A
T E N S E Z I E V A S Y N O N Y M
C I P O T P V S R R S Z K G U D O
P H R A S E E G E P F F V N M N X
```

Reading & Math Practice, Grade 6 © 2014 Scholastic Inc.

Number Place

Write each in standard form.

12 hundred thousandths _____

60 and 9 hundredths _____

47 ten-thousandths _____

7 thousand and 22 thousandths _____

Fast Math

Find each product mentally.

$10^1 \times 0.02 =$ $10^1 \times 0.063 =$ $10^2 \times 0.04 =$ $10^2 \times 0.2 =$

_____   _____   _____   _____

$10^1 \times 0.007 =$ $10^3 \times 0.003 =$ $10^3 \times 3.024 =$ $10^2 \times 5.047 =$

_____   _____   _____   _____

Think Tank

The weight of a bag of chips is labeled 6.5 ounces. This weight has been rounded to the nearest tenth of an ounce. What is the least that the actual weight of the bag could be?

_____

Show your work in the tank.

Data Place

The map shows the mileage from Juniper to Cranberry.
Lena left Juniper with 14 gallons in her car's gas tank.
She ran out of gas 5 miles past Huckleberry.
How many miles per gallon did Lena's car get on this trip? _____

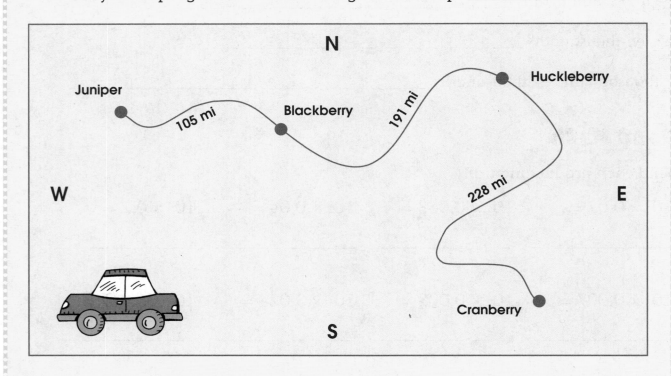

Puzzler

Yu wants to place 10 small round tables along the four walls of a square room so that each of the walls has the same number of tables.

Draw a sketch to show how he can do this.

Reading & Math Practice, Grade 6 © 2014 Scholastic Inc.

WORD of the Day

Use the word below in a short paragraph about an athlete.

strapping: (adj.) *tall, strong, and healthy*

_____

_____

_____

Sentence Mender

Rewrite the sentence to make it correct.

The buryal taked place at the Cemetary on Thirsday.

_____

Cursive Quote

Copy the quotation in cursive writing.

The greatest gift is not being afraid to question.

—Ruby Dee

- -

- -

- -

Is it? What do you think? Write your answer in cursive on another sheet of paper.

Analogy of the Day

Complete the analogy.

Stew is to **thick** as _____ is to **dense**.

○ A. soup   ○ B. hot   ○ C. desert   ○ D. jungle

Explain how the analogy works: _____

_____

📖 Ready, Set, READ!

Read the passage. Then answer the questions.

"We had visitors." For some, that would explain the pyramids, giant stone heads, designs on the desert floor, and other ancient works. Those who think this will tell you that past cultures did not have the technological know-how to construct massive monuments like pyramids and giant heads. They will insist that someone else or something else had to have built them. That's what they will claim. Take the giant Nazca lines in Peru, for example.

"It was extraterrestrials," they'll say. They say this because the high desert inhabitants had no reason to make lines and designs that could be seen from above. On the other hand, space travelers did. They wanted landing strips for their spaceships. The lines in the desert were runways for an airport.

Others have a different explanation for those ancient achievements. They'll argue that earthlings certainly did build all the marvels that we see today. They'll explain that they did so using very many workers and basic rules of physics and engineering.

You have read two views. What do you think: Human or Martian?

1. Why would people believe that visitors from space built some of the wonders of the ancient world? _____

_____

2. What view do you think the author of this passage believes?

_____

_____

🌀 BrainTeaser 🌀

Each sentence below has two blanks. Both use the same letters to form two _different_ words. Complete each sentence.

1. Tilt the _____ so it stands at a better _____ .

2. A leather _____ safely _____ a dog but lets her move.

3. A _____ must _____ dozens of eggs a day on the job.

4. Please position your _____ _____ the desk.

5. I rode the _____ along the rocky _____ .

6. She hopes the juice _____ won't ruin her _____ blouse.

Reading & Math Practice, Grade 6 © 2014 Scholastic Inc.

Number Place

Round each number to the nearest 1,000 *and* 100,000.

Number	Nearest 1,000	Nearest 100,000
389,900		
1,844,938		
24,061,562		

Fast Math

Divide.

$$100 \overline{)0.17} \qquad 22 \overline{)13.2} \qquad 4 \overline{)8.792} \qquad 0.1 \overline{)237}$$

Think Tank

Jake gets the oil changed in his car every 3,500 miles. He had his last oil change done at 34,792.4 miles. What will his car's odometer read when he has his next oil change?

_____

Show your work in the tank.

Data Place

The table shows official weights, in ounces, of some balls for sporting events.

Use the data to answer the questions.

Ball	Weight Range
softball	6.25–7.0
squash	0.821–0.912
tennis	2.0–2.06
croquet	15.75–16.25
volleyball	9.17–9.88
table tennis	0.085–0.09

1. To the nearest tenth of an ounce, what is the least a softball can weigh?

   _____

2. To the nearest tenth, how heavy can a volleyball be?

   _____

3. In which sport can a ball weighing 16 ounces be used? _____

4. Can an official tennis ball weigh 2.1 ounces? _____

5. Which ball weighs about $\frac{1}{10}$ of what a squash ball weighs? _____

Puzzler

Use the numbers 40, 4, and 162 to fill in the blanks in the sentences below in a way that makes sense. Then answer the question.

All _____ students in the sixth grade are going by bus to the play.

Will _____ buses be enough if each bus can take _____ students?

_____

_____

WORD of the Day

Use the word below in a short paragraph about a teacher, a class, or an assignment.

rigorous: (adj.) *severe; strict; harsh; thoroughly logical and scientific*

_____

_____

_____

Sentence Mender

Rewrite the sentence to make it correct.

We dissented the stares rapid-like during the firedrill.

_____

Cursive Quote

Copy the quotation in cursive writing.

Worries go down better with soup than without.

—Jewish proverb

_____

_____

_____

Is this a serious piece of advice? What do you think? Write your answer in cursive on another sheet of paper.

Analogy of the Day

Complete the analogy.

Bird is to **nest** as _____ is to **library**.

○ A. auditorium   ○ B. book   ○ C. building   ○ D. talking

Explain how the analogy works: _____

_____

 Ready, Set, READ!

Read the passage. Then answer the questions.

High heels have been around for centuries. At first, they were functional. The advantage of having them was appreciated by horseback riders who used them to secure their boots in stirrups. And elevated heels helped people in the Middle Ages get a few inches above the abundant waste in the streets. But it was in France in the 17th century that heels came into fashion. Men led the way.

This fad was begun by the Sun King, Louis XIV. He was powerful, but he was short. He decided to add inches to the heels of his shoes. To imitate him, the nobles had their boot makers do the same. When Louis had his shoes raised even higher, so did they.

Louis XIV

Starting in the next century, women's heels began to surpass men's heels in height and became commonly worn. American women followed the lead of the French and wore what was known as the "French heel." Over time, their heels got higher and narrower while those that men wore got shorter. By the early part of the 20th century, the term "high heel" did not refer to a shoe's height, but to a female footwear fashion. And that's how it is today.

1. How did elevated heels benefit people in the Middle Ages?

_____

_____

2. Explain why Louis XIV had his shoes raised even higher.

_____

_____

⑨ BrainTeaser ⑥

Put a ✓ in the box to show whether the word names one thing or more than one. If you can't tell, ✓ the last box.

Word	1 thing	2 or more	Can't tell
1. goose			
2. mice			
3. radio			
4. women			
5. scissors			
6. grapefruit			
7. headquarters			
8. cattle			

Reading & Math Practice, Grade 6 © 2014 Scholastic Inc.

Number Place

Round to the place of the underlined digit.

30,9̲48,007 _____   92,807.0̲45 _____

1,286,000.3̲72 _____   4,000,040̲,706 _____

8,726,739.02̲83 _____   5,528,90̲8,282 _____

Fast Math

Divide.

$0.001 \overline{)\ 0.8\ }$ $0.01 \overline{)\ 1.56\ }$ $0.4 \overline{)\ 0.76\ }$ $0.8 \overline{)\ 0.5\ }$

Compare. Write **<**, **=**, or **>**.

7 ÷ 8 _____ 1   14.3 ÷ 8 _____ 1   41.1 ÷ 0.99 _____ 1

Think Tank

Carmela's room is a rectangle. Its length is 5.5 yards and its width is 12.3 feet. It has a 9.25-foot ceiling. What is the perimeter of her room?

_____

Show your work in the tank.

Data Place

Students were asked to name their favorite T-shirt color. The table shows the results of the survey.

Make a double bar graph to display the data.

Color	Girls	Boys
White	4	7
Blue	8	8
Red	14	13
Green	7	5
Black	9	10

Favorite T-Shirt Colors

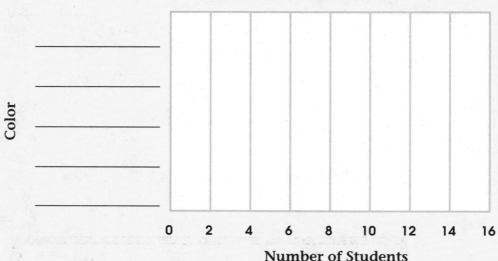

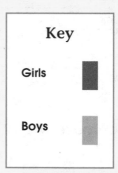

Key

Girls

Boys

Color

0 2 4 6 8 10 12 14 16

Number of Students

Describe what your graph shows. _____

_____

Puzzler

Finn is a fussy eater. Among the foods he will eat are corn, sprouts, beef, and muffins. He will never eat tuna, taco, cheese, or ravioli. Which will he eat—a pancake or a biscuit? _____

Explain. _____

_____

WORD of the Day

Use the word below in a short paragraph about a time you felt shame after something you or someone else did.

wither: (v.) *lose freshness; dry up; shrivel; feel or cause someone to feel ashamed or humiliated*

_____

_____

_____

Sentence Mender

Rewrite the sentence to make it correct.

We seen a scrawny kitten what needed food bad.

_____

Cursive Quote

Copy the quotation in cursive writing.

As I came to power peacefully, so shall I keep it.

—Corazon Aquino

_____

_____

_____

What do you think this means? Write your answer in cursive on another sheet of paper.

Analogy of the Day

Complete the analogy.

War is to **destruction** as _____ is to **fever**.

○ A. sickness   ○ B. temperature   ○ C. hay   ○ D. headache

Explain how the analogy works: _____

_____

Ready, Set, READ!

Read the passage. Then answer the questions.

A *fable* is a short story that teaches a lesson. Fables usually have animals and objects acting and speaking as humans would. "The Tortoise and the Hare" is a familiar one, and one of hundreds credited to the storyteller Aesop. His fables have been told and retold. They have been revised and translated into many languages. But who was Aesop? Did he write the fables? Where was he from? When did he live? Was he a Greek slave? Was he black? Did he even exist?

The answer to all those questions is that we don't really know. Different ancient thinkers had different views. Aristotle wrote that Aesop was from Thrace on the Black Sea coast. The historian Herodotus wrote that he was once a slave on the Greek island of Samos. And some of the characters in his stories suggested that Aesop was black. In fact, he has been portrayed as such more than once on television. In one production, he was played by comedian Bill Cosby.

But what matters most is not the answers to those biographical questions. It is that the fables have enriched lives around the world for millennia, and are as relevant today as they ever were.

1. What background information is known about Aesop?

_____

_____

2. Why does the author believe that such data is of small importance?

_____

_____

๑ BrainTeaser ๑

Write *a, e, i, o, u,* or *y* to finish spelling each instrument word.

1. c ____ ll ____

2. b ____ ss ____ ____ n

3. cl ____ r ____ n ____ t

4. m ____ r ____ mb ____

5. p ____ cc ____ l ____

6. m ____ nd ____ l ____ n

7. ____ k ____ l ____ l ____

8. ____ cc ____ rd ____ ____ n

9. s ____ x ____ ph ____ n ____

10. h ____ rm ____ n ____ c ____

Number Place

Round to the greatest nonzero place.

0.047 _____   9.807 _____

0.00872 _____   44.8123 _____

6,727.39 _____   0.00526 _____

Fast Math →

Divide.

$2.1 \overline{)0.063}$ $9 \overline{)0.099}$ $0.2 \overline{)0.03}$ $0.032 \overline{)0.8}$

💡 Think Tank

Dean hiked 22.8 kilometers. Dawn hiked 0.6 as far. How much farther than Dawn did Dean hike?

_____

Show your work in the tank.

Data Place

One way to rate baseball players is by comparing their batting averages. To compute a player's batting average, you divide hits by times at bat. Batting averages are generally rounded to three decimal places and do not have a zero before the decimal point.

Complete this batting average table. Then answer the questions.

Player	Hits	At-bats	Batting Average
Jackson	5	40	
Ruiz		90	.300
Morita	46		.250
Hunter		120	.400
Sullivan	26	60	

1. Which player has gotten a hit every 4 at-bats? _____

2. Which has gotten a hit every 2 out of 5 times at bat? _____

3. Sullivan wants to get his average up to .500.
   How many hits will he need in his next 10 at-bats? _____

Puzzler

Use the digits within the number bank *once* each to complete every number sentence.

Number Bank

3   7   8   1   4

1. ☐ ☐ ☐ – ☐ ☐ = 53

2. ☐ ☐ × ☐ ☐ + ☐ = 3,355

3. ☐ ☐ × ☐ ☐ ☐ = 17,808

WORD of the Day

Use the word below in a short paragraph about a fantasy or false impression.

illusion: (n.) *a false idea, perception, or impression*

_____

_____

_____

Sentence Mender

Rewrite the sentence to make it correct.

Do you sea a dr regular.

_____

Cursive Quote

Copy the quotation in cursive writing.

No one in the world needs a mink coat but a mink.

—Anonymous

_____

_____

_____

What does this mean? Write your answer in cursive on another sheet of paper.

Analogy of the Day

Complete the analogy.

Roof is to **house** as _____ is to **television**.

○ A. room   ○ B. couch   ○ C. repairs   ○ D. screen

Explain how the analogy works: _____

_____

📖 Ready, Set, READ!

Read the passage. Then answer the questions.

You've probably heard the saying *no pain, no gain.* Well, when it comes to being fit, that is not necessarily so. The simple, gentle, low-impact exercise of walking can ease you into a high level of fitness and health. Anyone can do it, even without belonging to a gym. There is no practice required.

Walking several times a week has many benefits. To begin with, it is good for your heart. In fact, regular brisk walks can reduce the risk of heart attack by the same amount as regular jogging. It's also good for your brain. Walking can make you smarter. And any fitness instructor will tell you how good walking is for managing your weight.

Walking is great for your health. It raises "good" cholesterol and lowers "bad" cholesterol. It lowers blood pressure. It reduces the risk of diabetes. And it improves your mood, too. How about that!

Walking is a form of exercise and you should treat it as such—prepare. Wear comfortable shoes and loose-fitting clothes. (Wear bright colors at night.) Stretch your calf and hamstring muscles before you begin. Then start slowly, to warm up and get into a comfortable stride. Then keep it up for as long as you wish.

1. Explain the meaning of the saying *no pain, no gain* in your own words.

   _____

   _____

   _____

   _____

2. What are the advantages of walking over jogging?

   _____

   _____

   _____

   _____

3. How could you recognize a comfortable stride?

   _____

   _____

   _____

   _____

🌀 BrainTeaser 🌀

Complete the category chart. The letters above each column tell the first letter for each word. One word is done for you.

	C	O	R	D
Sports		orienteering		
Birds				
States				
Rivers				

Reading & Math Practice, Grade 6 © 2014 Scholastic Inc.

Number Place

Solve.

I am the largest number in ten-thousandths that rounds to 0.683.

What number am I? _____

I am the smallest number in thousandths that rounds to 124.76.

What number am I? _____

Fast Math

Complete.

$28 + 8 = 4(\underline{} + 2)$

$5(3 + \underline{}) = 15 + 40$

$56 - 35 = \underline{}(8 - 5)$

$21 + 7 = 7(3 + \underline{})$

$36 - 8 = 4(\underline{} - 2)$

$3(11 + 15) = 33 + \underline{}$

Think Tank

Lefty and Pete divided 724.9 meters of fencing into 100 equal sections. How long is each section?

_____

Show your work in the tank.

Data Place

Use the diagram to answer the questions.

1. How many stars are common to the circle and square, but not the triangle?

    _____

2. How many stars are common to the circle and triangle, but not the square?

    _____

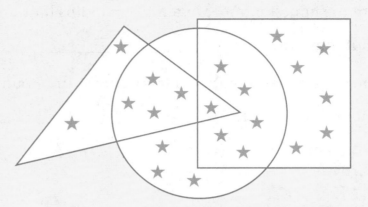

3. How many stars are common to all three figures? _____

4. How many stars are in only one of the three figures? _____

Puzzler

Look at the picture at the left. One picture in the row includes the first picture in the same position. Circle it.

1.

2.

WORD of the Day

Use the word below in a short paragraph about a shrill sound you might hear while hiking in nature or walking in a city.

strident: (adj.) *harsh and unpleasant sounding; shrill*

_____

_____

_____

Sentence Mender

Rewrite the sentence to make it correct.

The baseball teems cocaptains Carlos and Kim be hitting like babe ruth.

_____

Cursive Quote

Copy the quotation in cursive writing.

We do not remember days; we remember moments.

—Caesare Pavese

Is there a moment you remember well? Write about it in cursive on another sheet of paper.

Analogy of the Day

Complete the analogy.

Pediatrician is to **doctor** as _____ is to **scientist**.

○ A. optometrist   ○ B. laboratory   ○ C. science   ○ D. biologist

Explain how the analogy works: _____

_____

📖 Ready, Set, READ!

Read the story. Then answer the questions.

Uncle Sid looked and acted like the successful businessman he was. His business was trophy making. Chances are if you won something in our town, your trophy came from Uncle Sid's factory.

On Sundays our family would gather at Uncle Sid's spacious house. I enjoyed these occasions. Since my father died when I was a toddler, my uncles paid a lot of extra attention to me on those Sundays. But the main thing was that at each visit, I thought I would learn when Uncle Sid was finally going to take me fishing. He'd promised me innumerable times. Fishing! It was his idea, not mine. Rather than roughhousing with my cousins, I'd hover nearby and wait. He'd promised, so I persisted in believing that each Sunday would be the one when he'd put down his cigar, pinch my cheek, and say, "Okay, kiddo, I'll pick you up tomorrow early and we'll go out in the boat. What do you say?"

I would've said, "You bet!" But I never got the chance. Now, years later, this childhood disappointment has become a long-standing and bittersweet family joke. When one of us promises to do something, another of us will invariably say, "You're not going to Uncle Sid us now, are you?" I know I never will.

1. What most excited the author about the family gatherings?

   _____
   _____
   _____
   _____
   _____
   _____

2. How would you describe the tone of this remembrance?

   _____
   _____
   _____
   _____
   _____
   _____

🌀 BrainTeaser 🌀

Unscramble all ten words so they end with a long-*a* sound.
The hints in the box are out of order, but may offer help.

1. ILE _____

2. PYRE _____

3. EDYAC _____

4. WIGHE _____

5. TUBFEF _____

6. CHICLE _____

7. TIMENAE _____

8. IMEPOPI _____

HINTS
- ancient city buried in volcanic ash
- rot
- flower necklace
- hunted animal
- afternoon show
- tired expression
- help-yourself meal
- measure in pounds

Reading & Math Practice, Grade 6 © 2014 Scholastic Inc.

Number Place

Find the greatest common factor (GCF) of each set of numbers.

8, 24 _____   15, 35 _____

12, 18 _____   6, 9, 12 _____

5, 12, 14 _____   39, 104 _____

What two numbers between 10 and 20 have 6 as their GCF? _____

What two numbers between 18 and 30 have 8 as their GCF? _____

Fast Math

Round to the nearest whole number to estimate each sum or difference.

$9\frac{7}{8} - \frac{4}{5} =$ _____

$\frac{9}{10} + 1\frac{5}{7} =$ _____

$8\frac{1}{8} + 5\frac{1}{6} =$ _____

$2\frac{3}{4} + \frac{1}{6} =$ _____

$12\frac{2}{3} - 4\frac{5}{8} =$ _____

$\frac{7}{9} - \frac{5}{8} =$ _____

Think Tank

Remi buys some cashews and $2\frac{1}{4}$ pounds of almonds. He buys $5\frac{1}{8}$ pounds of nuts in all. How many pounds of cashews does he buy?

_____

Show your work in the tank.

Data Place

The line graph shows pizza sales at Vinnie's one week.

Use the data to answer the questions.

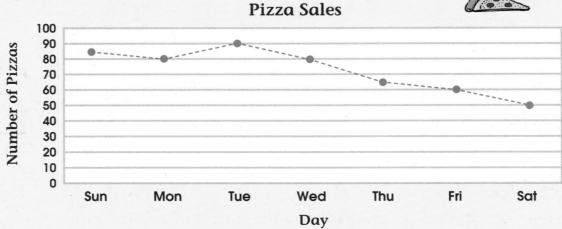

1. How many pizzas did Vinnie's sell on Monday? _____

2. Between which two days did the sales drop by 15? _____

3. How many pizzas did Vinnie's sell from Tuesday through Thursday? _____

4. How would you describe the changing pizza sales during the week?

_____

5. What might explain the change? _____

Puzzler

In the magic square, the sum for every row, column, and diagonal is $5\frac{1}{6}$.

Complete the magic square using fractions from the number bank. One fraction is not used.

Number Bank			
$\frac{3}{4}$	$1\frac{1}{12}$	$1\frac{1}{6}$	$1\frac{1}{4}$
$1\frac{5}{12}$	$1\frac{1}{2}$	$1\frac{3}{4}$	$1\frac{11}{12}$

$1\frac{2}{3}$		$1\frac{1}{6}$	$1\frac{7}{12}$
		$\frac{2}{3}$	
$\frac{11}{12}$	$1\frac{5}{6}$		1
	$1\frac{1}{3}$		$\frac{5}{6}$

WORD of the Day

Use the word below in a short paragraph about a time you or someone you know moved.

vacate: (v.) *go away from and leave empty or unoccupied; make vacant; make void*

_____

_____

_____

Sentence Mender

Rewrite the sentence to make it correct.

Hey come back this minute ewe rascle, yelled Jed.

_____

Cursive Quote

Copy the quotation in cursive writing.

Cherishing children is the mark of a civilized society.

—Joan Ganz Cooney

_____

_____

_____

What is another mark of a civilized society? Write your answer in cursive on another sheet of paper.

Analogy of the Day

Complete the analogy.

Doorbell is to **ring** as _____ is to **caw.**

○ A. finger   ○ B. crow   ○ C. duck   ○ D. doormat

Explain how the analogy works: _____

_____

📖 Ready, Set, READ!

Read the passage. Then answer the questions.

For the sixth-grade science fair, I chose to explore the idea of hydroponics. Hydroponics is the growing of plants in water with nutrients, but without the use of soil. Using this method, scientists can grow plants in inhospitable places like the arctic, the desert, or in a spaceship.

I bought three plants, all the same kind and size. I potted one of them in soil and watered it regularly. I potted one in sand and watered it regularly, too. I set the roots of the third plant in water enhanced with the nutrients soil would otherwise provide. I put all three plants on the same windowsill so each got the same amount of sun.

I measured plant heights every day. I observed that after two weeks, the plant in the sand was alive, but not healthy. The plant in the soil had grown nicely. But the plant in the enriched water grew to be the tallest and hardiest of the three.

I constructed a line graph to compare plant growth, and I provided a list of all materials and the added nutrients. My reward: a first-place prize!

1. What is hydroponics? _____

_____

2. What information about the experiment did the writer leave out?

_____

_____

3. What was the result of the experiment? _____

_____

🌀 BrainTeaser 🌀

Write all the different words you can spell using three or more letters from the word *incomprehensible*.

_____

_____

_____

_____

_____

Reading & Math Practice, Grade 6 © 2014 Scholastic Inc.

Number Place

Find the least common multiple (LCM) of each set of numbers.

3, 4 _____   2, 5 _____   40, 16 _____

10, 12 _____   5, 6, 12 _____   8, 9, 10 _____

7, 8, 56 _____   5, 9, 27 _____   8, 13, 52 _____

Fast Math

Find each sum or difference in simplest form.

$\frac{5}{6} - \frac{1}{3} =$ _____ $\frac{3}{8} + \frac{5}{24} =$ _____ $3\frac{7}{8} + 3\frac{1}{2} =$ _____

$\frac{7}{8} - \frac{4}{5} =$ _____ $6 - 4\frac{1}{8} =$ _____ $10\frac{3}{8} - 7\frac{5}{8} =$ _____

$9\frac{1}{12} - 5\frac{3}{8} - 1\frac{3}{4} =$ _____ $15\frac{5}{6} + 12\frac{7}{9} =$ _____

Think Tank

The same number is added to the numerator and denominator of a fraction less than 1. Will the new fraction formed be less than, equal to, or greater than the original one? Explain.

_____

_____

_____

Show your work in the tank.

Data Place

The histogram shows the number of text messages sixth graders sent one Saturday.

Use the data to answer the questions.

Text Messages Sent

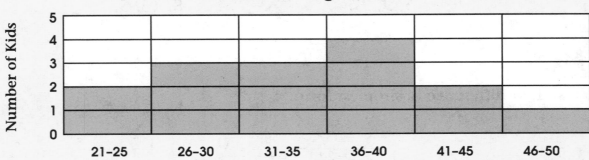

Number of Kids (vertical axis: 0, 1, 2, 3, 4, 5)

Number of Messages (horizontal axis: 21–25, 26–30, 31–35, 36–40, 41–45, 46–50)

1. How many kids sent between 46 and 50 messages? _____

2. How many kids sent fewer than 36 messages? _____

3. How many more kids sent between 36 and 40 messages than sent between 21 and 25 messages? _____

4. What is the mode of the data? _____ How can you tell?

_____

Puzzler

Use one number from the triangle and one from the circle to answer the questions.

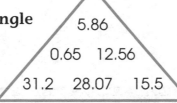

Triangle: 5.86 0.65 12.56 31.2 28.07 15.5

Circle: 1.08 4.92 2.5 1.468 12.14 19.4

1. Which two numbers have a sum of 13.64? _____

2. Which two numbers have a difference of 11.8? _____

3. Which two numbers have a sum of 18 and a difference of 13? _____

Reading & Math Practice, Grade 6 © 2014 Scholastic Inc.

WORD of the Day

Use the word below in a short paragraph about a career you might choose.

vocation: (n.) *occupation, business, profession, or trade; a special calling*

_____

_____

_____

Sentence Mender

Rewrite the sentence to make it correct.

If you want something dun. Ax a bizzy person.

_____

Cursive Quote

Copy the quotation in cursive writing.

Nothing pains some people more than having to think.

—Dr. Martin Luther King, Jr.

_____

_____

_____

What did the author mean by this? Write your answer in cursive on another sheet of paper.

Analogy of the Day

Complete the analogy.

Fork is to **eat** as _____ is to **unlock**.

○ A. lock   ○ B. door   ○ C. key   ○ D. spoon

Explain how the analogy works: _____

_____

📖 Ready, Set, READ!

Read the passage. Then answer the questions.

Did it get its start in the Netherlands 900 years ago? Did it have its beginnings in China a few hundred years earlier? Or did it evolve in Scotland during the Middle Ages? The origin of the hugely popular sport of golf is much debated.

Stick and ball games had been around for centuries. The 18-hole version of the sport is generally thought to have been a Scottish invention The term golf probably comes from the Dutch word *kolf*, meaning "club."

The first official mention of golf was in a 1457 act of the Scottish Parliament. It prohibited playing *gowf* and football at a time when archery practice was seen as far more important. Other restrictions on the "unprofitable" game of golf followed. But so did many examples of royals playing the game.

In 1687, the earliest known golf instructions appeared. But the sport did not gain in popularity until the late 19th century. Today, in many parts of this country and others, you can't drive very far without passing a golf course. In 2016, after an absence of 112 years, this ancient sport will again be an Olympic event.

1. What can you deduce from the fact that royals played golf despite restrictions?

_____

_____

2. What does *unprofitable* mean in this context?

_____

_____

🌀 BrainTeaser 🌀

Each word below starts and ends with the same letter.
But every missing letter pair is different.
Complete the words.

1. ____ rom ____

2. ____ eapo ____

3. ____ ido ____

4. ____ leri ____

5. ____ oggi ____

6. ____ verd ____

7. ____ icku ____

8. ____ ende ____

9. ____ urpas ____

Number Place

Write whether the fraction is closest to 0, $\frac{1}{2}$, or 1.

$\frac{1}{8}$ _____ $\frac{13}{15}$ _____ $\frac{5}{8}$ _____ $\frac{7}{10}$ _____

$\frac{2}{9}$ _____ $\frac{9}{20}$ _____ $\frac{17}{28}$ _____ $\frac{1}{3}$ _____

Complete. Write a fraction that is equal to or close to $\frac{1}{2}$.

$\frac{n}{11}$ _____ $\frac{n}{15}$ _____ $\frac{9}{n}$ _____ $\frac{n}{9}$ _____

$\frac{n}{27}$ _____ $\frac{4}{n}$ _____ $\frac{n}{21}$ _____ $\frac{15}{n}$ _____

Fast Math

Find each product in simplest form.

$\frac{12}{20} \times \frac{5}{6} =$ _____ $\frac{3}{4} \times \frac{2}{9} =$ _____ $\frac{2}{3} \times 18 =$ _____

$3\frac{1}{7} \times 4\frac{2}{3} =$ _____ $4\frac{1}{6} \times 12 =$ _____ $\frac{5}{9} \times 2\frac{1}{4} =$ _____

Think Tank

The box LaShawni's TV came in measures 6 feet by $4\frac{1}{2}$ feet, by $8\frac{1}{2}$ inches. What is the volume of the box in cubic feet?

_____

Show your work in the tank.

Data Place

Rocco's Tacos is all the rage. After waiting in a long line, you can choose from many one-of-a-kind fillings. And Rocco's prices—hardly rock-bottom!

Use the menu to answer the questions.

Ketchup and Tuna Taco	$15.95
Lamb and Lint Taco	$18.95
Tadpole Taco (add 50¢ for special pond sauce)	$12.50
Stallion and Rice Taco	$15.25
All Desserts (ice cream only)	$8.95
All Sides (rice or beans only)	$6.75
All Drinks	$4.00

1. Sam orders the stallion and rice taco, a side, and a drink. He pays with two $20 bills. What will his change be? _____

2. Ivanka orders the most expensive taco and two sides. She has $15 OFF coupon. Can she also buy a dessert if she has $25? Explain.

   _____

3. Annie spent $30 on her meal, including a $4.05 tip. She ordered three things. What did she order?

   _____

Puzzler

Try this handshake problem.

Twelve players entered the video game tournament. Each player shook hands with every other player. How many handshakes were there?

Hint: Use simpler numbers and look for a pattern.

WORD of the Day

Use the word below in a short paragraph about being clumsy.

bumbling: (adj.) *clumsy; stumbling; awkward*

_____

_____

_____

Sentence Mender

Rewrite the sentence to make it correct.

My friend one the essay contest but to me Frans peace was the best.

_____

Cursive Quote

Copy the quotation in cursive writing.

The first rule of holes: when you're in one, stop digging.

—Molly Ivins

_____

_____

_____

What did Ivins mean by this clever observation? Write your answer in cursive on another sheet of paper.

Analogy of the Day

Complete the analogy.

Puppy is to **cute** as _____ is to **sticky**.

○ A. kitten   ○ B. flypaper   ○ C. water   ○ D. sandpaper

Explain how the analogy works: _____

_____

📖 Ready, Set, READ!

Read the passage. Then answer the questions.

For any right triangle, the sum of the squares of its legs equals the square of its hypotenuse: $a^2 + b^2 = c^2$. This is the *Pythagorean Theorem*. It is credited to the ancient Greek philosopher, astronomer, and religious thinker Pythagoras, and is what he is best remembered for to this day.

Pythagoras was born about 2,600 years ago on the island of Samos. He was a lifelong teacher who began by tutoring just a few students by making and coloring shapes in sand. For Pythagoras, proof mattered above all else. Two angles were not equal simply because they looked to be the same size. Their congruence had to be proven.

Pythagoras was unappreciated during his lifetime. His practices seemed strange and threatening. For instance, he taught both men and women at a time when women in Greece were forbidden to attend any kind of gathering. Once, an angry mob burned down his meeting places and he had to flee for his life. But his work influenced later thinkers and his ideas spread. Today, all geometry students around the world work with concepts Pythagoras discovered.

1. Why did the methods Pythagoras used seem threatening?

_____

2. Some think that the theorem is not the work of Pythagoras but of one of his successors. Why might there be uncertainty? _____

_____

🌀 BrainTeaser 🌀

Use each clue to complete a word that starts with *lim*.

1. kind of bean   LIM ____
2. stagger   LIM ____
3. arms or legs   LIM ____ ____
4. boundary   LIM ____ ____
5. flexible, like a dancer   LIM ____ ____ ____
6. kind of poem   LIM ____ ____ ____ ____ ____
7. rock used for building   LIM ____ ____ ____ ____ ____ ____
8. fancy car with driver   LIM ____ ____ ____ ____ ____ ____

Reading & Math Practice, Grade 6 © 2014 Scholastic Inc.

Number Place

Write the number in standard form.

1×10^2 _____ 10^4 _____ $10^3 + 10^2$ _____

3×10^3 _____ 10^6 _____ $5^2 + 10^4$ _____

Fast Math

Rename each unit of measure.

40 ft = _____ yd   114 in = _____ ft   8 gal = _____ qt

80 oz = _____ lb   50 fl oz = _____ c   4 T = _____ lb

Compare. Write **<**, **=**, or **>**.

7 gal _____ 29 qt   7 pt 5 c _____ 19 c   33 pt _____ 16 qt 1pt

10 c _____ 6 pt   15 yd _____ 50 ft   4.5 T _____ 10,000 lb

Think Tank

A freight train is half a mile long. It travels at a speed of 60 mph. It comes to a tunnel that is 1 mile long. How long will it take the train to pass completely through?

_____

Show your work in the tank.

Data Place

Some students at Galileo School have projects on display in the science fair. The graph shows how many students from each grade have their work on display.

Use the data to answer the questions.

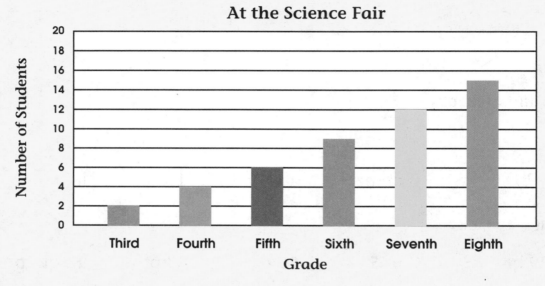

At the Science Fair

1. How many students have projects on display? _____

2. How many more 7th graders than 5th graders have projects at the fair? _____

3. What fraction of the student scientists are in 8th grade? _____

4. What fraction are in the highest three grades? _____

5. Which two grades together make up $\frac{1}{3}$ of the students with projects on display?

_____

Puzzler

Laura used the following shortcut to quickly find the sum of all numbers from 1 to 10. Study what she did:

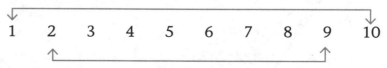

Use Laura's shortcut to find the sum of all numbers from 1 to 100. Explain the method.

_____

_____

Reading & Math Practice, Grade 6 © 2014 Scholastic Inc.

WORD of the Day

Use the word below in a short paragraph about a place you would like to stay for a while.

tarry: (v.) *delay leaving; linger; stay for a while; dawdle*

_____

_____

_____

Sentence Mender

Rewrite the sentence to make it correct.

Swamps, Marshes, Bogs all wetlands.

_____

Cursive Quote

Copy the quotation in cursive writing.

He is always right who suspects that he makes mistakes.

—Anonymous

_____

_____

_____

Do you think this is or is not true? Explain. Write your answer in cursive on another sheet of paper.

Analogy of the Day

Complete the analogy.

Maroon is to **color** as _____ is to **music**.

○ A. classical   ○ B. stage   ○ C. instrument   ○ D. island

Explain how the analogy works: _____

_____

📖 Ready, Set, READ!

Read the passage. Then answer the questions.

Columbus was sad to report that he hadn't come across a single monster during his voyage. He feared for his reputation. This was not a frivolous concern. Explorers in those days expected to come across horrible monsters in their travels.

Long before Columbus set sail, mariners regularly claimed to have discovered odd creatures and fantastical islands. People were fascinated by these adventure yarns. They were as popular then as superhero adventures are today. And those tales were full of whoppers!

For centuries, dozens of fake islands found their way onto maps. It took centuries more for mapmakers to remove them. But even as maps improved, eager explorers continued to search for imaginary places. Even the savvy French navigator Jacques Cartier was susceptible. He heard about a paradise full of gold and inhabited by winged men. He wasted months looking for it.

Progress eventually put to rest most myths of imaginary lands and their bizarre inhabitants. But it takes time to dismiss legends. If you doubt this, consider the Loch Ness monster. The first mention of this creature took place 1,500 years ago!

1. Why did Columbus feel a sense of disappointment? _____

_____

2. Why did it take so long for mapmakers to correct old errors?

_____

_____

🌀 BrainTeaser 🌀

Homophones are words that sound the same but have different spellings and meanings.

Write the correct word in each sentence.

1. She is the drummer of her _____.   **band** *or* **banned**

2. He won his first silver _____.   **medal** *or* **meddle**

3. That was a very _____ dream!   **bazaar** *or* **bizarre**

4. Duct tape works well for _____.   **ceiling** *or* **sealing**

5. Lucia buys homemade _____ jam.   **currant** *or* **current**

6. It's time, _____ you're ready or not.   **weather** *or* **whether**

7. Our _____ wear red caps.   **assistance** *or* **assistants**

Reading & Math Practice, Grade 6 © 2014 Scholastic Inc.

Number Place

Solve.

What is the greatest even number you can make that is greater than 5,000,000,000 and less than 6,000,000,000?

_____

What is the greatest number that rounds to 1 billion when rounded to the nearest million?

_____

Fast Math

Rename each unit of measure.

6 cm = _____ m   9.7 km = _____ m   4.8 m = _____ cm

19 g = _____ mg   0.768 L = _____ mL   621 mg = _____ g

Compare. Write <, =, or >.

0.45 m ___ 45 cm   8.8 km ___ 880 m   24 L ___ 240 mL

24 g ___ 240 mg   1.55 kg ___ 1,550 g   3,100 mL ___ 3 L

💡 Think Tank

City A reported 1.45 m of rain. City B reported 139.5 cm of rain. Which city had more rain? Explain.

_____

_____

_____

_____

Show your work in the tank.

Data Place

The information on the gas pumps tells the price per gallon.

Use this price information to answer the questions. Round your answers to the nearest cent.

Regular
$3.49

1. **Greg's car**
   Tank capacity: 18 gal
   Gallons left: 8.6

   Gallons used: _____

   Cost to fill tank with regular gasoline:

   _____

Diesel
$3.09

2. **Camille's car**
   Tank capacity: 24 gal
   Gallons left: 4.7

   Gallons used: _____

   Cost to fill tank with diesel gasoline:

   _____

3. Greg has a coupon for $\frac{1}{10}$ off the price of regular. What will it cost to fill the rest of his tank with that discount? _____

Puzzler

Try this penny problem.

Suppose you have 1,000,000 pennies. If you could stack them on top of one other, about how high would the stack reach?

Hint: You don't need to make the whole stack to make a sensible estimate.

94

WORD of the Day

Use the word below in a short paragraph about calming down someone who is upset or angry.

pacify: (v.) *make peaceful or calm; bring under control*

_____

_____

_____

Sentence Mender

Rewrite the sentence to make it correct.

I think it were Elena left their backpack on the bus.

_____

Cursive Quote

Copy the quotation in cursive writing.

It's not how good you are. It's how good you want to be.

—Paul Arden

_____

_____

_____

Do you agree? Explain why. Write your answer in cursive on another sheet of paper.

Analogy of the Day

Complete the analogy.

Bake is to **eat** as _____ is to **grow**.

○ A. plant   ○ B. tree   ○ C. bread   ○ D. dirt

Explain how the analogy works: _____

_____

📖 Ready, Set, READ!

Read the e-mail. Then answer the questions.

Dear Grandma,

We got in yesterday really late and it was already dark. I thought we'd never arrive. But when I awoke this morning, smelled the fragrant tropical flowers outside our front door, and saw the awesome turquoise waters, I smiled from ear to ear. (The color REALLY is like it looks on the postcard Kevin sent you.) Mom says we are in paradise. And I don't even mind Kevin (even though he is as annoying as ever!)

Earlier today, Dad and I went snorkeling. It was TOTALLY AMAZING! It was like having a floodlight shining on everything in sight underwater. I saw fish of all shapes and colors. I spotted beautiful coral, too. Whole schools of fish fanned by me on all sides. I saw see-through fish, chubby little fish, and long, skinny ones with pointed snouts. I think I even saw a baby octopus.

Well, now it's nearly time for dinner. We're eating grilled shrimp on the beach. Kevin will probably whine for his peanut butter and jelly. I don't care. I'm having a great time. It's TOTALLY COOL here. You'd love it. Hug Grandpa for me.

Miss you so much!
Love, Maureen

1. Where is the family vacationing?
   - ○ A. at a ski resort
   - ○ B. on a safari
   - ○ C. on a tropical island
   - ○ D. in the nation's capital

2. What is the tone of this e-mail?
   - ○ A. informational
   - ○ B. gleeful
   - ○ C. bored
   - ○ D. terse

3. What does the author mean by saying "it was like having a floodlight shining on everything"?

   _____

   _____

   _____

   _____

   _____

🌀 BrainTeaser 🌀

Unscramble each gem word below. Write it correctly in the spaces.
Then unscramble the boxed letters to name
the hardest natural substance on earth. _____

1. RIPHEAPS ___ ☐ ___ ___ ___ ☐ ___ ___

2. TRANGE ___ ___ ___ ☐ ___ ___

3. PAZTO ☐ ___ ___ ___ ___

4. REDMALE ___ ☐ ___ ___ ___ ___ ☐

5. DEJA ___ ☐ ___ ___

Reading & Math Practice, Grade 6 © 2014 Scholastic Inc.

Number Place

Compare. Write <, =, or >.

585,500,000 _____ 585,005,000

300,000,099,000 _____ 300,001,000,000

1,000,000,370,000 _____ one trillion thirty-seven thousand

four hundred fifty trillion _____ 450,000,000,000

Fast Math

Solve for *n*.

$\frac{1}{2} \div \frac{1}{4} = n$ _____

$\frac{2}{5} \div \frac{1}{10} = n$ _____

$\frac{6}{8} \div \frac{3}{8} = n$ _____

$n = \frac{2}{5} \div \frac{2}{5}$ _____

$n = \frac{9}{10} \div \frac{6}{7}$ _____

$\frac{1}{8} \div \frac{1}{5} = n$ _____

$n = \frac{2}{9} \div \frac{1}{3}$ _____

$n = \frac{6}{13} \div \frac{3}{26}$ _____

$\frac{1}{11} \div \frac{1}{6} = n$ _____

Think Tank

A cubic foot of water weighs $62\frac{1}{2}$ pounds. What is the weight of $5\frac{1}{3}$ cubic feet of water?

_____

Show your work in the tank.

Data Place

Frank's Fruits is an online fruit delivery business.

Place your order and wait for the doorbell to ring.

Use the price list to fill the food orders.

Frank's Fabulous Prices	
Peaches	$1.28/lb
Bananas	$.79/lb
Grapes	$1.99/lb
Limes	5 for $1
Apples	$1.40/lb

1.5 lb apples
2 lb bananas
15 limes

3.5 lb apples
$\frac{3}{4}$ lb peaches
$\frac{1}{2}$ doz. limes

1. Total price: _____

2. Total price: _____

Puzzler

The cake at the right is in the shape of a rectangle.

1. Using 3 straight cuts, what is the greatest number of pieces of cake you can make?

_____

2. What is the greatest number of pieces you can make with 4 straight cuts?

_____

Hint: The pieces of cake do not have to be of equal size.

WORD of the Day

Use the word below in a short paragraph about a grumpy person.

crotchety: (adj.) *cranky, grouchy, or ill-tempered; full of odd whims*

_____

_____

_____

Sentence Mender

Rewrite the sentence to make it correct.

Hay what you doing with my lap top.

_____

Cursive Quote

Copy the quotation in cursive writing.

No one can make you feel inferior without your consent.

—Joseph Joubert

_____

_____

_____

What did Joubert mean by this? Write your answer in cursive on another sheet of paper.

Analogy of the Day

Complete the analogy.

Bumbling is to **clumsy** as _____ is to **challenging**.

○ A. stumbling   ○ B. easy   ○ C. rock climbing   ○ D. rigorous

Explain how the analogy works: _____

_____

📖 Ready, Set, READ!

Read the recipe. Then answer the questions.

Here is how to make delicious French toast for two.

Ingredients

2 eggs	cinnamon
¼ cup milk	butter
salt	4 slices of bread

1. Crack the eggs into a bowl. Add the milk. Use a fork to mix it in with the eggs. Add a pinch of salt and a dash of cinnamon. Stir until blended.

2. Melt a pat of butter on the skillet. Keep the skillet on medium heat.

3. Dip the bread into the egg mixture, one slice at a time.

4. Put the slices on the heated skillet. Flip after one side browns. Repeat as needed.

5. Serve with any topping you enjoy—maple syrup, fresh fruit, yogurt, or nuts.

1. What utensils must you gather? _____

_____

2. How many eggs would you need to make 16 slices of French toast?

_____

3. Which ingredients are optional? _____

_____

🌀 BrainTeaser 🌀

An *anagram* is a new word made using all the letters of another word. *Sore* is an anagram for *rose*.

Make an anagram for each word.

1. spine ⇔ _____   5. cellar ⇔ _____

2. panel ⇔ _____   6. stifle ⇔ _____

3. sever ⇔ _____   7. rental ⇔ _____

4. stream ⇔ _____   8. meteor ⇔ _____

Number Place

Write each of the following.

an expression with *factors* 3 and *y* _____

an expression with a *coefficient* of 7 _____

an expression for a number decreased by 6 _____

an expression that is the *quotient* of *w* and 4 _____

an expression for 10 more than a number _____

Fast Math

Find each quotient.

$9 \div \frac{3}{7} =$ _____

$27 \div \frac{3}{5} =$ _____

$\frac{7}{15} \div 42 =$ _____

$84 \div 5\frac{1}{4} =$ _____

$3\frac{1}{2} \div \frac{1}{3} =$ _____

$6 \div 2\frac{1}{4} =$ _____

$3\frac{1}{4} \div 1\frac{1}{2} =$ _____

$5\frac{1}{7} \div 2\frac{1}{7} =$ _____

$4\frac{4}{5} \div 1\frac{1}{5} =$ _____

Think Tank

Sixty-four kids play in a single-elimination chess tournament. That means that one loss knocks a player out of the competition. How many games will it take to determine the winner of the chess tournament?

_____

Show your work in the tank.

Data Place

The map of Canine County is graphed on a coordinate grid.

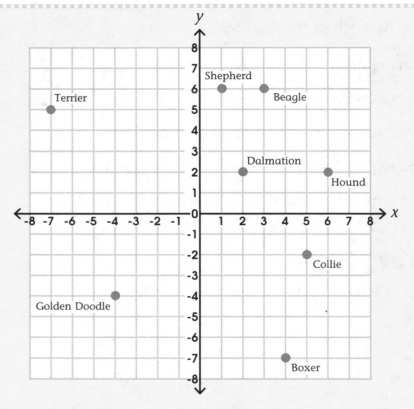

Use the information on the grid to answer the questions.

1. In which quadrant will you find each town?

   Beagle _____   Terrier _____   Golden Doodle _____

2. What are the coordinates for each town?

   Shepherd _____   Collie _____   Hound _____

3. Which town is located at (4, –7)? _____

   In which quadrant is that town? _____

Puzzler

Place as many smiley faces as you can in the grid without getting three in a row vertically, horizontally, or diagonally.

Reading & Math Practice, Grade 6 © 2014 Scholastic Inc.

WORD of the Day

Use the word below in a short paragraph about something that has been renovated.

refurbish: (v.) *polish up again; brighten; restore or improve*

_____

_____

_____

Sentence Mender

Rewrite the sentence to make it correct.

The coach see that he need to have the players practice more oftenly.

_____

Cursive Quote

Copy the quotation in cursive writing.

Continuous improvement is better than delayed perfection.

—Mark Twain

Do you agree? Explain. Write your answer in cursive on another sheet of paper.

Analogy of the Day

Complete the analogy.

Fish is to **school** as _____ is to **faculty**.

○ A. jury   ○ B. guppy   ○ C. professor   ○ D. student

Explain how the analogy works: _____

_____

Ready, Set, READ!

Read the passage. Then answer the questions.

Who do you know who has sideburns? Sideburns are patches of facial hair grown on the side of the face near the ears. They are as common as beards and mustaches. Although men may have been wearing these side-whiskers on and off for centuries, the name is a relatively recent one.

Side whiskers went in and out of fashion for centuries. They were popularized anew by European soldiers during Napoleon's time. The style spread to the young nation of America. Look at paintings of President Andrew Jackson or of others of his time and you will see the style. But the facial hair was not yet called sideburns. We can thank a Civil War general for the change.

Union General Ambrose P. Burnside's appearance was distinguished by long, thick side whiskers from his ears to his cheeks and linked by a mustache. He was beardless. His style launched a trend. The term "burnsides" was used to describe facial hair like his. About 50 years after the war, the word got transposed. Burnsides became sideburns.

1. What are sideburns? _____

_____

2. How does the photo help you better visualize Burnside's appearance?

_____

_____

BrainTeaser

Write an antonym from the word bank for each boldface word below.

1. **immense** responsibility _____

2. **recede** into the fog _____

3. **encompass** the area _____

4. **diversity** of interests _____

5. **gloat** about it _____

6. **slake** my thirst _____

7. **devastate** the town _____

8. a **petty** argument _____

Word Bank

mourn
minute
serious
exclude
develop
increase
advance
sameness

Reading & Math Practice, Grade 6 © 2014 Scholastic Inc.

Number Place
. . . .

Write the value of the variable.

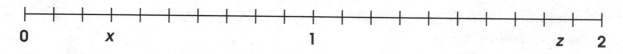

$X =$ _____ $Z =$ _____

Fast Math

Find the range, mean, median, and mode for each set of numbers.

| 3 | 8 | 7 | 12 | 6 | 8 | 14 | 8 | 6 |

range = _____   mean = _____   median = _____   mode = _____

| 62 | 44 | 78 | 57 | 59 |

range = _____   mean = _____   median = _____   mode = _____

Think Tank
. . . .

On her math tests, Shonda scored 82 once, 85 six times, 90 seven times, and 94 four times. What are the range, mean, median, and mode of her test scores?

_____

_____

_____

_____

Show your work in the tank.

Data Place

The table shows heights, in inches, of students in Mr. Tahl's class.

Make a histogram to display the data.
Give the graph a title.

Height (in Inches)	Frequency
49–52	2
53–56	3
57–60	4
61–64	7
65–68	3
69–72	1

Frequency

Height (in Inches)

Puzzler

Here is a pattern that folds to form a number cube. What are the sums of the numbers on opposite faces of that cube?

_____

_____

_____

3.7	4.9
1.9	

2.3	4.6
	3.0

WORD of the Day

Use the word below in a short paragraph about a place that makes you feel safe and protected.

sanctuary: (n.) *a sacred place; a place that provides refuge or protection*

_____

_____

_____

Sentence Mender

Rewrite the sentence to make it correct.

The Taj Mahal, in india, maybe the World's more famous toom.

_____

Cursive Quote

Copy the quotation in cursive writing.

I have always imagined that paradise will be a kind of library.

—Jorge Luis Borges

_____

_____

_____

What does this quotation reveal about Borges? Write your answer in cursive on another sheet of paper.

Analogy of the Day

Complete the analogy.

Scale is to **weigh** as _____ is to **cook**.

○ A. sink   ○ B. frying pan   ○ C. spoon   ○ D. table

Explain how the analogy works: _____

_____

Ready, Set, READ!

Read the following ad for a new brand of carpet spot remover. Then answer the questions.

No stain too tough! No job too big! *Spot-Off* is spot-on!

Spot-Off is the answer to your rug stain problems.

- Removes almost every kind of stain in seconds.
  Grape juice—no worry! Chocolate ice cream—not a problem!
  Coffee stains—bring 'em on!

- In the words of our satisfied customers:
  "a miracle" "worked like magic" "a wonder" "best I've tried"

- Try our product. If you're not completely satisfied you'll get your money back.

- Look for *Spot-Off* in top stores. Hurry while the supply lasts!

Don't believe everything you read in an advertisement. Write three questions you might ask the advertiser to challenge the claims for this product.

1. _____

   _____

2. _____

   _____

3. _____

   _____

⊚ BrainTeaser ⊚

The word wheel holds nine letters. If you use all nine of them, you can form a nine-letter word. Then form other words (from three to eight letters) always using the E in the center and any others.

_____

_____

_____

_____

Reading & Math Practice, Grade 6 © 2014 Scholastic Inc.

Number Place

Write the missing numbers.

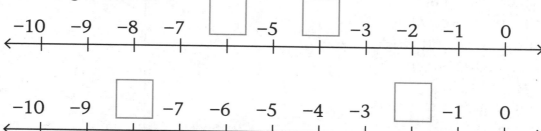

Fast Math

Find the range, mean, median, and mode for each set of numbers.

| $2.03 | $2.46 | $2.35 | $2.35 | $2.91 |

range = _____   mean = _____   median = _____   mode = _____

| $3\frac{1}{2}$ | $\frac{5}{8}$ | $\frac{3}{4}$ | $1\frac{1}{8}$ | $2\frac{3}{8}$ |

range = _____   mean = _____   median = _____   mode = _____

Think Tank

Ted opened his social studies textbook. When Bo asked him to what pages his book was opened, he answered that the product of the facing pages was 87,912. To what pages did Ted open his book?

_____

Show your work in the tank.

Data Place

The map of the sea floor is graphed on a coordinate grid. Each letter on the grid marks the location of a sunken ship.

Each small square on the grid has an area of 1 mi².

Use the grid to answer the questions.

1. Which ship is 6 miles west of ship A? _____

2. Which ship is 5 miles east of ship E? _____

3. Which ship is 7 miles west, 11 miles south of ship B? _____

4. Which ship is 6 miles east, 4 miles north of ship E? _____

5. Which ship is directly northeast of ship F? _____

Puzzler

The six bags below contain either coffee, tea, or cocoa. Only one bag contains tea. There is twice as much coffee as cocoa. What is the weight of the bag that holds the tea? _____

6 lb   7 lb   9 lb

5 lb   3 lb   4 lb

WORD of the Day

Use the word below in a short paragraph about a person trying hard to reach a goal.

dogged: (adj.) *not giving up; stubbornly determined; persistent*

_____

_____

_____

Sentence Mender

Rewrite the sentence to make it correct.

The lindsay Twins look alike and don't thinks alike.

_____

Cursive Quote

Copy the quotation in cursive writing.

How old would you be if you didn't know how old you are?

—Satchel Paige

Well, how old *would* you be? Write your answer in cursive on another sheet of paper.

Analogy of the Day

Complete the analogy.

Foil is to **assist** as _____ is to **fallible**.

○ A. edible   ○ B. tin   ○ C. unreliable   ○ D. unerring

Explain how the analogy works: _____

_____

📖 Ready, Set, READ!

Read the passage. Then answer the questions.

You would think that the Civil War would have been enough to occupy Americans in the 1860s. Huge armies were fighting. Factories were busy producing uniforms, bullets, guns, wagons, and ships. But all the while, two "armies" of men were part of another large national project. They were building a railroad that would link the two coasts.

At that time, railroads from the East reached only to Nebraska. One army of workers started from there. A second began in California. The race to meet up was on. Thousands of men laid track as fast as they could. Irish immigrants, free blacks, and Chinese workers labored side by side. By 1869, their grueling job was done. The tracks from the East met the tracks from the West in Utah. It had taken only seven years. Telegraph lines buzzed with the remarkable news. The entire continent now could be crossed by rail!

Constructing a transcontinental railroad through rough terrain and blasting tunnels through mountains was backbreaking work. Meeting that challenge was the engineering achievement of the century.

1. What did the armies of workers achieve? _____

_____

2. What made their job so hard? _____

_____

3. Explain the meaning of *transcontinental.* _____

_____

🌀 BrainTeaser 🌀

Use the clues to complete each word that includes *qu*.

1. exactly the same   ____ Q U ____ ____

2. tight-knit social group   ____ ____ ____ Q U ____

3. crush   ____ Q U ____ ____ ____

4. opposite of solid   ____ ____ Q U ____ ____

5. tennis tool with strings   ____ ____ ____ Q U ____ ____

6. happening often   ____ ____ ____ Q U ____ ____ ____

7. speaking expressively   ____ ____ ____ Q U ____ ____ ____

8. peaceful, serene   ____ ____ ____ ____ Q U ____ ____

Number Place

Write the integer that represents each of the following:

a loss of $5 dollars _____

an increase in altitude of 400 feet _____

a dive to 75 feet below sea level _____

a rise in temperature of 6 degrees _____

Fast Math

Write each expression as an algebraic expression. Use *n* as the variable.

a number increased by 7 _____

a number decreased by 2.8 _____

eight more than a number squared _____

the product of a number and 12 _____

Think Tank

Li visited the city. First, she spent one-fourth of her money on breakfast in the train station. Then she spent one-half of what she had left on a train ticket. When she got to the city, she spent one-half of what remained on a taxi to the museum, where she examined her finances over a $2 iced tea. She had only $5.50 left! How much money did Li have with her when she started the day?

_____

Show your work in the tank.

Data Place

Mia is training to run a 5-kilometer race. The graph shows the distances she ran during one week of training.

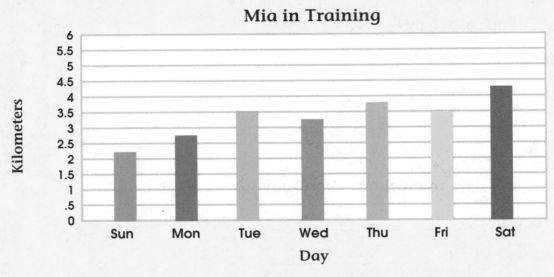

Mia in Training

Use the graph to make up reasonable questions that fit the answers below.

1. **A:** Wednesday and Thursday

    Q: _____

2. **A:** 0.5 kilometers

    Q: _____

3. **A:** 2 kilometers

    Q: _____

Puzzler

Draw a line segment across the clock so that the sums of the numbers on both sides of the line segment are the same.

What is that sum? _____

Reading & Math Practice, Grade 6 © 2014 Scholastic Inc.

WORD of the Day

Use the word below in a short paragraph about a time you or someone you know was being nosy.

pry: (v.) *pull loose by force; look with curiosity; be inquisitive or nosy about something*

_____

_____

_____

Sentence Mender

Rewrite the sentence to make it correct.

working one in one with a math tooter were very helpfull.

_____

Cursive Quote

Copy the quotation in cursive writing.

It is easier to build strong children than to repair broken men.

—Frederick Douglass

....

....

....

What did the former slave and great leader and orator mean by this observation? Write your answer in cursive on another sheet of paper.

Analogy of the Day

Complete the analogy.

Dawn is to **morning** as _____ is to **evening**.

○ A. night   ○ B. dusk   ○ C. dark   ○ D. midnight

Explain how the analogy works: _____

_____

📖 Ready, Set, READ!

Read the fable from Nigeria. Then answer the questions.

The chief was having a huge feast. There would be joyous music and dancing. Messengers scurried from house to house to invite all his people to come. Each guest was asked to bring a calabash of wine.

One man wanted very badly to come, but had no wine to bring. But, he thought, if hundreds of people poured their wine into the chief's huge pot, who would notice if just one calabash had water instead of wine? So that's what he decided to do.

The day of the great feast arrived. All guests had donned their finest clothes. As guests entered the chief's home, they poured their calabashes into the chief's giant pot. The man did the same when it was his turn.

After all guests had arrived, the chief's servants walked about the large room and filled everyone's cup with wine from the pot. But when the man and the other guest put their cups to their lips to drink, they were very disappointed to taste only water.

1. What is a *calabash*?

_____

_____

_____

_____

_____

_____

2. What lesson does this fable teach?

_____

_____

_____

_____

_____

_____

🌀 BrainTeaser 🌀

Write *a, e, i, o, u,* or *y* to complete each baseball word.

1. p ____ nn ____ nt

2. b ____ llp ____ rk

3. ____ ____ tf ____ ____ ld

4. pl ____ ____ ____ ffs

5. sh ____ t ____ ____ t

6. s ____ cr ____ f ____ c ____

7. d ____ v ____ s ____ ____ n

8. st ____ t ____ st ____ c

9. r ____ l ____ ____ v ____ r

10. l ____ ____ g ____ ____

Number Place

What inequality is shown? Use *n* as the variable.

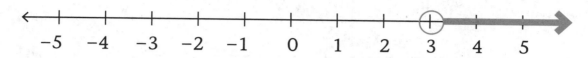

_____

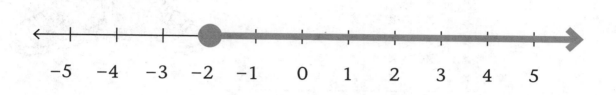

_____

Fast Math

Write each expression as an algebraic expression. Use *n* as the variable.

3 more than twice a number _____

three times a number decreased by 4^2 _____

5 less than twice a number _____

the sum of 8.5 and 2.5 times a number _____

a squared number multiplied by 45 _____

Think Tank

Jack weighs *n* pounds. He carries two packages. One weighs 10 pounds, the other, *d* pounds. Write an expression for the total weight, in pounds, of the two packages.

_____

Show your work in the tank.

Data Place

The line plot shows the sneaker sizes of all the members of the school baseball team.

Sneaker Sizes

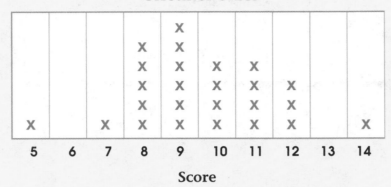

| 5 | 6 | 7 | 8 | 9 | 10 | 11 | 12 | 13 | 14 |

Score

The team's equipment manager made the line plot from data she collected and recorded in a frequency table.

Show what that table would look like. Then summarize what the data shows.

_____

_____

_____

Sneaker Size	Tally	Frequency

Puzzler

This hexagon consists of six line segments. How many new line segments can you draw to connect all the vertices?

_____

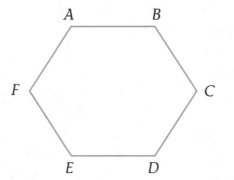

Reading & Math Practice, Grade 6 © 2014 Scholastic Inc.

WORD of the Day

Use the word below in a short paragraph about something you find baffling.

enigma: (n.) *something or someone that is extremely puzzling; that which cannot be understood or explained*

_____

_____

_____

Sentence Mender

Rewrite the sentence to make it correct.

Both her and me had mist the deadline for reports but it hurt our grades.

_____

Cursive Quote

Copy the quotation in cursive writing.

Always make the best of the best, and never make bad worse.

—Earl of Chesterfield

_____

_____

_____

Is this good advice? Explain why in cursive on another sheet of paper.

Analogy of the Day

Complete the analogy.

Knife is to **sharp** as _____ is to **slick**.

○ A. sand   ○ B. dull   ○ C. oil   ○ D. cut

Explain how the analogy works: _____

_____

Ready, Set, READ!

Read the poem. Then answer the questions.

The Lake Isle of Innisfree
by W.B. Yeats

I will arise and go now, and go to Innisfree,
And a small cabin build there, of clay and wattles made:
Nine bean-rows will I have there, a hive for the honeybee,
And live alone in the bee-loud glade.

And I shall have some peace there, for peace comes dropping slow,
Dropping from the veils of the morning to where the cricket sings;
There midnight's all a glimmer, and noon a purple glow,
And evening full of the linnet's wings.

I will arise and go now, for always night and day
I hear lake water lapping with low sounds by the shore;
While I stand on the roadway, or on the pavements grey,
I hear it in the deep heart's core.

1. What does the speaker want most to find at Innisfree?

_____

_____

2. Give two examples of how the poet uses language to create a vivid image of Innisfree.

_____

_____

BrainTeaser

Did you see where the computer hackers ran?

Solve each clue. Then copy each letter into its numbered box to find the answer to the riddle. One letter has been done for you.

• Four times five

$\overline{\hspace{1em}}_{11}$ $\overline{\hspace{1em}}_{13}$ $\overline{\hspace{1em}}_{3}$ $\overline{\hspace{1em}}_{7}$ $\overline{\text{T}}_{8}$ $\overline{\hspace{1em}}_{15}$

• Opposite of birth

$\overline{\hspace{1em}}_{9}$ $\overline{\hspace{1em}}_{6}$ $\overline{\hspace{1em}}_{10}$ $\overline{\hspace{1em}}_{1}$ $\overline{\hspace{1em}}_{2}$

• Not here

$\overline{\hspace{1em}}_{12}$ $\overline{\hspace{1em}}_{5}$ $\overline{\hspace{1em}}_{14}$ $\overline{\hspace{1em}}_{4}$

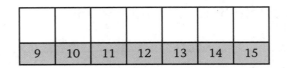

1	2	3	4

5	6	7	8

9	10	11	12	13	14	15

120

Reading & Math Practice, Grade 6 © 2014 Scholastic Inc.

Number Place

What inequality is shown? Use *m* as the variable.

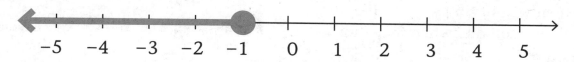

_____

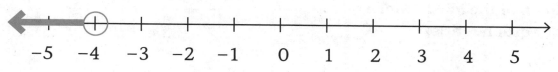

_____

Fast Math

Evaluate each expression for *n* = 4.

$3 + n$ _____ $5.5n$ _____ $7 - n$ _____

$2n + 6$ _____ $\frac{n}{4}$ _____ $n^2 - 5$ _____

$n^2 + n + 7.5$ _____ $3n - 8$ _____ $15 - 2.5n$ _____

Think Tank

Seda cycled 142.5 miles in *y* days. She cycled the same distance each day. Write an expression for the distance she cycled each day.

_____

Show your work in the tank.

Data Place

Four friends joined a track team. The table shows their weights in pounds when they began the season and when they finished it.

Display the data in a horizontal double bar graph. Choose numbers for the x axis and add all of the labels. Make a key. Give your graph a title.

Person	Start Weight	Finish Weight
Kiley	110	103
Marcus	104	101
Amir	126	117.5
Toni	84.5	80

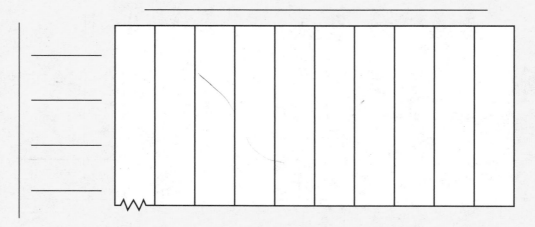

Key

Start ☐

Finish ☐

1. How can you tell who lost the most weight? _____

2. How can you tell who lost the greatest fraction of his or her starting weight?

_____

Puzzler

Fill in the eight squares with the numbers 1–8 so that no two consecutive numbers are connected by a line segment. Use each number once only.

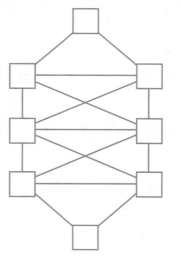

WORD of the Day

Use the word below in a short paragraph about a time you were very hungry, and what you did about it.

famished: (adj.) *suffering severely from hunger; starving*

I blinked my eyes, washing away the blur of a midnight nightmare. I grab the glass cup. The moonlight hits it and twinkles like a thousand stars! My somewhat ornate sheet seems dim and colourless. I grab the edge and pull it of my body. Famished, my bare feet grip my now black looking carpet. I grab my doorframe and stare into the pitch black hallway. I move around the most creaky floor boards. I quickly open the cupboard. I grab a tortilla. It feels tender soft and fresh between my ice cold fingers. I take a bite and head back to my room. When I'm in bed and comfortable I feed myself again.

Sentence Mender

Rewrite the sentence to make it correct.

Monica opened the winder this mourning and looks out.

Cursive Quote

Copy the quotation in cursive writing.

You grow up the day you have your first real laugh—at yourself.

—Ethel Barrymore

You grow up the day you have your first laugh, at yourself

Ethel Barrymore

Do you agree? Why? Write your answer in cursive on another sheet of paper.

Analogy of the Day

Complete the analogy.

Stage is to **theater** as _____ is to **book**.

○ A. binding   ○ B. reader   ○ C. writer   ○ D. orchestra

Explain how the analogy works: _____

_____

📖 Ready, Set, READ!

Read the passage. Then answer the questions.

The toy has two disks connected to an axle; a length of string loops around the axle. Napoleon's soldiers played with richly decorated versions of it, as Europeans had been doing for two centuries. It was popular in the Philippines for several centuries. And there is indisputable evidence—a picture on a bowl showing a boy playing with one—that the ancient Greeks enjoyed it 2,500 years ago. But it might have gotten its start even earlier than that, in China.

Although there is no easy answer to where and when the yo-yo was invented, we do know that two people were responsible for popularizing the modern version of it here in America. Those two were Pedro Flores and Donald Duncan.

Flores came here from the Philippines. In the 1920s, he improved the toy by having it come to rest at the end of the string and then return upward. He began manufacturing yo-yos and inventing tricks to do with them. Duncan witnessed Flores's expert play and was impressed. He bought Flores's company. He spent a fortune to do so, but the yo-yo booms in the 1960s and 1990s made him wealthy. It made a lot of kids happy, too. You can learn more by visiting the Yo-Yo Museum's website.

1. Who was Pedro Flores, and what part did he play in the history of the yo-yo?

   _____

2. What early physical evidence does the author cite about the age of the yo-yo?

   _____

3. What information would you look for on the website for the Yo-Yo Museum?

   _____

🌀 BrainTeaser 🌀

Think of one word that all three words on the left have in common.
Write it on the line. This first one is done for you.

1. wagon
   cart
   Ferris — _wheel_

2. bread
   bushel
   hand — _____

3. skunk
   hair
   bug — _____

4. wedding
   twelfth
   sleepless — _____

5. river
   blood
   savings — _____

6. India
   invisible
   washable — _____

Reading & Math Practice, Grade 6 © 2014 Scholastic Inc.

Number Place

Write each fraction or mixed number as a decimal, and each decimal as a fraction or mixed number.

$\frac{9}{10}$ _____   0.06 _____

0.010 _____ $\frac{5}{100}$ _____

$1\frac{3}{1,000}$ _____   −4.01 _____

−0.014 _____   2.0003 _____

Fast Math

Evaluate each expression for $a = 0.75$ and $b = 2.06$.

$a + b + 8$ _____ $2(a + b)$ _____

$a + b - 2.2$ _____ $3a + 2b$ _____

$a + 4.55 - b$ _____ $(2a + b) \div 4$ _____

Think Tank

These clubs meet after school and on weekends. The glee club meets every third day. The chess club meets every fourth day. The photography club meets every sixth day. All three clubs met today, Thursday. On what day of the week will all three clubs again meet on the same day?

_____

Show your work in the tank.

Data Place

The map shows the four time zones in the U.S.A.

Use the map to answer the questions.

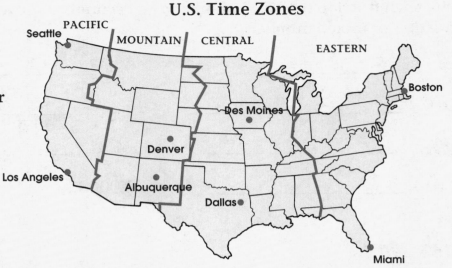

U.S. Time Zones

1. If it is 4:30 P.M. in Denver, what time is it in

   Seattle? _____ Dallas? _____ Miami? _____

2. If it is 7:00 A.M. in Boston, what time is it in

   Los Angeles? _____ Dallas? _____ Denver? _____

3. If it is 8:15 P.M. in Miami, what time is it in

   Boston? _____ Seattle? _____ Des Moines? _____

Puzzler

1. Reposition 2 toothpicks to make 7 squares.

2. Use 10 toothpicks to form 2 squares.

126

WORD of the Day

Use the word below in a short paragraph about something that would encourage you to study harder.

motivate: (v.) *provide with a reason for doing; provide with an incentive*

_____

_____

_____

Sentence Mender

Rewrite the sentence to make it correct.

Write after my birthday I cent out thank you notes.

_____

Cursive Quote

Copy the quotation in cursive writing.

Be not afraid of growing slowly; be afraid only of standing still.

—Chinese proverb

- -

- -

- -

What is the meaning of this proverb? Write your answer in cursive on another sheet of paper.

Analogy of the Day

Complete the analogy.

Guitar is to **musician** as _____ is to **diver.**

○ A. fish   ○ B. banjo   ○ C. sea   ○ D. mask

Explain how the analogy works: _____

_____

📖 Ready, Set, READ!

Read the passage. Then answer the questions.

If the deep canyons and red buttes of northern New Mexico were Georgia O'Keeffe country, the rugged forests of coastal British Columbia were Emily Carr country. What O'Keeffe's paintings did for the American Southwest, Carr's did for the Pacific Northwest. And like O'Keeffe, Carr succeeded against great odds.

Emily Carr was born in Victoria, British Columbia, in 1871. She was fascinated by the lives of the indigenous coastal people of Vancouver Island. She visited their remote villages and studied and wrote about their lives. She painted their villages and colorful totems. But it was her spirited landscapes and forest paintings for which she is best remembered.

Carr's painting style was influenced by that of Canada's Group of Seven, which included the country's best known modernist painters—all men. But unlike most members of the group, Carr painted in seclusion. For a while, she lived deep in the dense forest, in total isolation. But she was not alone; her pet monkey shared her tiny wooden trailer with her.

Emily Carr was an artistic pioneer at a time when few opportunities existed for independent women in the arts. Today, an art and design university in Canada bears her name.

1. Compare Georgia O'Keeffe and Emily Carr, based on the text.

_____

_____

_____

_____

2. Define *indigenous*. _____

_____

_____

_____

_____

3. Why might an artist choose to live and work in isolation?

_____

_____

_____

_____

_____

🌀 BrainTeaser 🌀

Grades is a flexible word. Rearrange its six letters and add one more to form new seven-letter words. Solve them using the hints below.

1. Add **b** for forest animals _____

2. Add **g** for sharp knives _____

3. Add **n** for hazards _____

4. Add **n** for flower beds _____

5. Add **p** for seized _____

6. Add **r** for good wishes _____

7. Add **u** for sweetened _____

Reading & Math Practice, Grade 6 © 2014 Scholastic Inc.

Number Place

Order the integers from *least* to *greatest*.

−6   −2   −9   −5   _____

−4   4   40   −40   _____

Order the integers from *greatest* to *least*.

−9   −91   19   9   _____

−17   7   −77   17   _____

Fast Math

Simplify each expression.

$7n - 2n$ _____ $n + 2n$ _____

$5n - 2n + 4n$ _____ $5n + 2n - 3s$ _____

$6y + (3y + 2)$ _____ $3(2t + 2t)$ _____

Think Tank

A set of golf clubs and a golf bag together cost $300. Golf balls cost $25 for a dozen. The clubs cost 4 times as much as the bag does. What does the bag cost?

_____

Show your work in the tank.

Data Place

Use the coordinate grid to graph the transformations below.

1. Graph each point and its translation. Write the coordinates of the translation.

    A (5, 4) left 2 units, up 3 units

    _____

    B (−3, 1) right 6 units, down 4 units

    _____

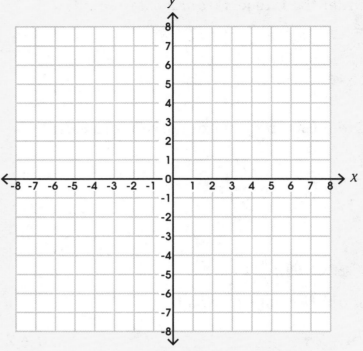

2. Graph triangle *EFG* and its image *E'F'G'*. Write whether the image is a reflection or a translation. Describe the transformation.

    Figure: *E* (−3, 0), *F* (0, 3), *G* (3, 0)   Image: *E'* (−2, −2), *F'* (1, 1), *G'* (4, −2)

    _____

    _____

Puzzler

Sylvia earns $9.60 an hour at her job. The clocks show when she punched in and when she punched out one afternoon. How much did she earn during that period of time?

_____

Reading & Math Practice, Grade 6 © 2014 Scholastic Inc.

WORD of the Day

Use the word below in a short paragraph about giving or getting thoughtful advice.

sage: (adj.) *showing good judgment; wise*

_____

_____

_____

Sentence Mender

Rewrite the sentence to make it correct.

Many of us realizes that soda candy and junk food is bad for hour health?

_____

Cursive Quote

Copy the quotation in cursive writing.

Don't be afraid to cry. It will free your mind of sorrowful thoughts.

—Hopi proverb

_____

_____

_____

What is your view of this proverb? Write your answer in cursive on another sheet of paper.

Analogy of the Day

Complete the analogy.

Rain is to **flooding** as _____ is to **laughter**.

○ A. sadness   ○ B. singing   ○ C. joke   ○ D. sunshine

Explain how the analogy works: _____

_____

📖 Ready, Set, READ!

Read the passage. Then answer the questions.

Famous sports writer Red Smith called him the best athlete "of any time in any land." To this day, many will agree.

Jim Thorpe grew up in Oklahoma, a Native American of Sauk, Fox, and Pottawatomie heritage. By the age of six, he could shoot, ride, trap, and go on long hunting treks. His breakfast of champions: fried squirrel. When he was older, he attended government-run Indian schools. At Carlisle Indian Industrial School, he excelled in football, baseball, track, and lacrosse. His coach was none other than *the* Pop Warner, the famous football coach who did much to popularize the game, especially for youngsters.

When Sweden's King Gustav V placed two gold medals around Thorpe's neck for winning the decathlon and pentathlon at the 1912 Olympics, he called him the greatest athlete in the world. Thorpe merely said, "Thanks." He didn't attend any celebrations. "I didn't want to be gazed upon as a curiosity," he added. Then the unexpected happened. The International Olympic Committee stripped Thorpe of his medals and removed his marks from the official records. Why? He had played professional minor league baseball.

The IOC was pressured over the years to give Thorpe the recognition he deserved. But Thorpe didn't care. "I won 'em and I know I won 'em," he told his daughter. Eventually, the reluctant committee did give replicas of the medals to his family. And his picture did eventually end up on boxes of breakfast cereal. But Jim Thorpe's results from 1912 are still not mentioned in official Olympic records.

Note: The 2012 U.S.A. Olympic basketball team was comprised totally of professional athletes.

1. What is your view on the 1912 IOC decision to strip Thorpe of his medals?

_____

_____

2. What does the author think about this? _____

_____

🌀 BrainTeaser 🌀

Pick an interesting person, place, or thing. Name it on the first line below. Then write 26 colorful adjectives you could use to describe your pick. Use every letter from *a* to *z*.

_____ is . . . _____

_____

Reading & Math Practice, Grade 6 © 2014 Scholastic Inc.

Number Place

Rename each pair of fractions using the LCD as their denominator.

$\frac{3}{5}$ and $\frac{1}{4}$

$\frac{9}{10}$ and $\frac{2}{5}$

$\frac{7}{12}$ and $\frac{9}{15}$

_____

_____

_____

Compare. Write <, =, or >.

$\frac{7}{8}$ ____ $\frac{9}{10}$

$\frac{5}{12}$ ____ $\frac{5}{9}$

$\frac{11}{21}$ ____ $\frac{33}{63}$

Fast Math

Write an equation for each statement.

A number w increased by 2.5 is equal to 3.8. _____

The difference between a number y and 82 is 47. _____

A number n divided by 0.5 is equal to 2. _____

The product of a number k and $\frac{3}{8}$ is $1\frac{7}{8}$. _____

Think Tank

Carlos took a 3-day car trip. On the second day he drove 360 miles. On the third day he drove 3 times as far as he did on the first day. If his trip was 1,080 miles long, how far did Carlos drive on the first day?

_____

Show your work in the tank.

Reading & Math Practice, Grade 6 © 2014 Scholastic Inc.

Data Place

The line plot shows heights, in stories, of buildings in Deb's town.

Use the data to answer the questions.

Building Heights

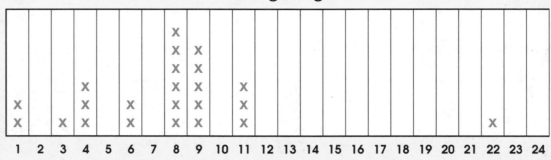

Number of Stories

1. How many buildings are listed in the plot? _____

2. What is the range of the data? _____

3. What is the mode of the data? _____

4. Where are the gaps in the data? _____

5. Which building height is an outlier? _____

Puzzler

In each shape, cross out the fraction or mixed number that does *not* belong.
Then, write one of your own that *does* belong on the line beneath the shape.

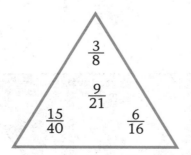

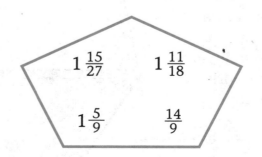

1. _____

2. _____

WORD of the Day

Use the word below in a short paragraph about an obstinate person.

headstrong: (adj.) *foolishly determined to have one's own way; stubborn; obstinate*

_____

_____

_____

Sentence Mender

Rewrite the sentence to make it correct.

"Climate" and "Weather" is two terms that often confused.

_____

Cursive Quote

Copy the quotation in cursive writing.

Only when you have eaten a lemon do you appreciate what sugar is.

—Ukrainian proverb

_____

_____

_____

What does this proverb mean? Explain. Write your answer in cursive on another sheet of paper.

Analogy of the Day

Complete the analogy.

Thoroughbred is to **horse** as _____ is to **sport**.

○ A. fan   ○ B. soccer   ○ C. stadium   ○ D. winning

Explain how the analogy works: _____

_____

📖 Ready, Set, READ!

Read the passage. Then answer the questions.

The Newbery Award is given each year to the author who has made the most distinguished contribution to children's literature. Margarita Engle won it in 2009 for her historical novel *The Surrender Tree*. Engle was the first Latina recipient of this prestigious award.

Engle was born and raised in Los Angeles, from where her American father hailed. But her family often spent summers in Cuba visiting her mother's relatives. There, Engle developed a strong bond with her extended family and fell in love with the country. She also grew to love tropical nature. In addition to focusing on creative writing, she has studied botany and crop production.

Engle says that writing historical fiction feels like "time travel." She says that it is a "dreamlike blend of imagination and reality." And she loves to write about "young people who make hopeful choices that seemed hopeless." *The Surrender Tree* is about Rosa, a young nurse in Cuba in 1896. Rosa makes difficult decisions in her effort to do what is right rather than what is safe during the troubled time of Cuba's revolution. Engle says that she hopes that "tales of courage and compassion will ring true for youthful readers as they make their own difficult decisions."

Today, Margarita Engle lives in central California. When she's not writing, she works with her husband, training rescue dogs.

1. What is the Newbery Award? _____

_____

2. How does the author's use of quotations give insights into the life and work of

Margarita Engle? _____

_____

🌀 BrainTeaser 🌀

Imagine a journey to any place in the world at any time, past, present, or future! Write 26 different verbs for actions, conditions, or experiences you might have along the way. Use each letter from *a* to *z*.

On my journey to _____ , I will _____

_____

_____

_____

Number Place

Order the fractions from *least* to *greatest*.

$\frac{5}{6}$ $\frac{5}{8}$ $\frac{7}{8}$ $\frac{6}{7}$ _____

$\frac{3}{5}$ $\frac{3}{8}$ $\frac{3}{10}$ $\frac{1}{2}$ _____

Order the numbers from *greatest* to *least*.

$\frac{7}{10}$ $\frac{10}{7}$ $1\frac{1}{7}$ 1 _____

$2\frac{2}{3}$ $2\frac{2}{5}$ $2\frac{3}{4}$ $2\frac{1}{2}$ _____

Fast Math

Solve.

$n + 119 = 254$ $n =$ _____

$23 + 76 = b$ $b =$ _____

$56 - t = 42$ $t =$ _____

$m + 11 + 17 = 44$ $m =$ _____

$0 + y = 13$ $y =$ _____

$316 + n = 401 + 226$ $n =$ _____

Think Tank

In its 5-day life, a bug ate 150 smaller bugs. Each day it ate 8 more bugs than it did the day before. How many bugs did it eat on the first day of its life?

_____

Show your work in the tank.

Data Place

The pictograph shows average home attendance at five ballparks.

Use the graph to answer the questions.

Average Home Game Attendance

Fanning Stadium	⚾ ⚾ ⚾ ◔
Fuller Field	⚾ ⚾ ⚾ ⚾ ⚾ ⚾ ◖
Clark Park	⚾ ⚾ ⚾ ⚾ ◖
M-T Stadium	⚾ ⚾ ◔
Wynn Field	⚾ ⚾ ⚾ ⚾ ⚾ ⚾ ⚾ ⚾
Key	⚾ = 6,000 fans

1. Which stadium had the greatest average home attendance? What was it?

   _____

2. Which stadium's average home attendance was 21,000 less than that of

   Wynn Field? _____

3. The average home attendance at Fanning Stadium was about two-fifths of that

   of which stadium? _____

4. Which stadium's average home attendance was closest to the mean of the data?

   _____

5. What is the mean absolute deviation of the attendance data? _____

Puzzler

This square is divided into four congruent rectangles.
Each rectangle has a perimeter of 20 units.
What is the perimeter and area of the square?

Perimeter: _____   Area: _____

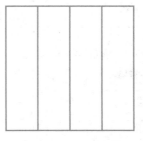

Reading & Math Practice, Grade 6 © 2014 Scholastic Inc.

WORD of the Day

Use the word below in a short paragraph about finding something unexpected in a basement, closet, or attic.

rummage: (v.) *search through by moving things about*

_____

_____

_____

Sentence Mender

Rewrite the sentence to make it correct.

There is cougar tracks ahead, but be carfull," the ranger warning.

_____

Cursive Quote

Copy the quotation in cursive writing.

The smallest good deed is better than the grandest good intention.

—Japanese proverb

....

....

....

....

Do you think this is right? Explain. Write your answer in cursive on another sheet of paper.

Analogy of the Day

Complete the analogy.

Optional is to **required** as _____ is to **energetic**.

○ A. sluggish   ○ B. voluntary   ○ C. lively   ○ D. puppy

Explain how the analogy works: _____

_____

Reading & Math Practice, Grade 6 © 2014 Scholastic Inc.

📖 Ready, Set, READ!

Read the e-mail. Then answer the questions.

Sent: Tue 12/10/2012
To: Stephan
Subject: Coaching

Hi Stephan,

Thanks for inviting me to coach the kids' soccer team. As much as I would love to, I need to turn you down. Sorry, pal, but my schedule has me out of town practically nonstop over the next few months. I'd miss too many games and practices. Wouldn't want to let the kids down by phoning it in!

Have you considered Gio's mom, Corrine? Or Sarah's dad, Don, who I think played for Cornell? Either would do at least as well as I would. I'm sure they would. After all, I am a little rusty.

So, good luck finding the right person. Wish I could've helped.

Scooooooooore!
Joao

1. Why does Joao turn down Stephan's offer? _____

_____

2. How would you describe the tone of this e-mail? _____

_____

3. What does Joao mean by writing that he's a *little rusty*?

_____

_____

🌀 BrainTeaser 🌀

The sentence in the box has only seven words.
But every word starts with the *same* letter.
Write a sentence in which every word begins with *R*.
Make it as long as you can.

> **D**octor **D**ouglas **d**elays **d**ifficult **d**ecisions **d**uring **d**aylight.

_____

_____

Number Place

Compare. Write **<**, **=**, or **>**.

2.005 _____ $2\frac{5}{100}$

3.7 _____ $3\frac{1}{7}$

4.20 _____ four and two hundredths

1.25 _____ $1\frac{1}{4}$

22.6 _____ $2\frac{2}{6}$

six and fifty thousandths _____ $6\frac{5}{100}$

Fast Math

Solve.

$38n = 760$ $\qquad$ $n =$ _____

$y \div 75 = 184$ $\qquad$ $y =$ _____

$200 = 80m$ $\qquad$ $m =$ _____

$17w = 255$ $\qquad$ $w =$ _____

$\frac{s}{15} = 120$ $\qquad$ $s =$ _____

$650 = p \div 13$ $\qquad$ $p =$ _____

Think Tank

You know the price of a week's pass to a gym. You also know the price of a yearly membership. How can you determine how much you would save in a year by buying the yearly membership rather than paying for one week at a time?

_____

_____

_____

_____

Show your work in the tank.

Data Place

The table shows scoring in a football league.

The Modem played the Drive.

Touchdown	6 points
Touchdown With Extra Point.	7 points
Field Goal	3 points
Safety.	2 points

Use the clues to fill in the scoreboard.
Then answer the question.

- At the end of the first quarter, the score was 10–7.
- At the end of the second quarter, the score was 15–16.
- At the end of the third quarter, the score was 32–29.
- At the end of the fourth quarter, the score was 41–43.
- The Modem had a field goal in each quarter, but only one safety in the game. It was in the second quarter.
- The Drive had at least 1 touchdown with extra point in each quarter.

Quarter	1	2	3	4	Final Score
Modem					
Drive					

Who won the game? _____

Puzzler

Show how you would use line segments to divide this figure into two figures having the same size and shape.

Reading & Math Practice, Grade 6 © 2014 Scholastic Inc.

WORD of the Day

Use the word below in a short paragraph about something that you believe will be remembered.

posterity: (n.) *all of a person's descendants; all future generations*

_____

_____

_____

Sentence Mender

Rewrite the sentence to make it correct.

Buying a good Dictionary may be the wiser investing a righter can make.

_____

Cursive Quote

Copy the quotation in cursive writing.

No matter what accomplishments you make, somebody helped you.

—Althea Gibson

_____

_____

_____

_____

What example supports or disputes this view? Write your answer in cursive on another sheet of paper.

Analogy of the Day

Complete the analogy.

Tall is to **towering** as _____ is to **fascinating**.

○ A. awesome   ○ B. short   ○ C. interesting   ○ D. boring

Explain how the analogy works: _____

_____

📖 Ready, Set, READ!

Read the passage. Then answer the questions.

Televised dance contests are very popular today. Millions tune in to watch celebrities and pros show their moves. They root for their favorites. It's all for fun and profit. But the dance marathons during the Great Depression were a horse of a different color. They were both wildly popular and highly controversial.

The dance marathons of the 1920s and '30s were endurance contests couples entered in hopes of earning much-needed cash. Amateurs competed alongside professionals. Contestants danced nonstop for hundreds of hours to win prize money. Bedraggled dance pairs walked, swayed, shuffled, and lugged one another across the floor. Often, one or both partners would collapse from exhaustion.

The rules stated that contestants had to remain in motion for 45 minutes of every hour. Staying in motion meant picking up one foot and then the other. Judges would walk the floor. They swatted contestants with rulers to keep them moving. If a dancer's knee touched the ground, it meant instant disqualification.

In their heyday, dance marathons were among America's most widely attended forms of live entertainment. Twenty-five cents allowed audiences to watch the contests for as long as they wished. What they saw was a grim spectacle indeed.

1. What does a *horse of a different color* mean? _____

_____

2. Why do you think the dance marathons were popular during the Great Depression?

_____

3. Why were the dance marathons *grim spectacles*? _____

_____

🌀 BrainTeaser 🌀

Climb the word ladder to change *candy* to *heart*. Change only one letter at a time. Write the new word on each rung.

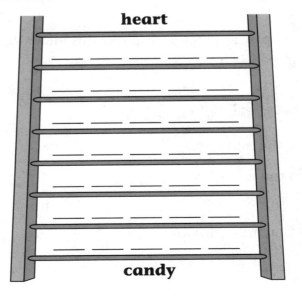

heart

candy

Reading & Math Practice, Grade 6 © 2014 Scholastic Inc.

Number Place

Compare. Write **<**, **=**, or **>**.

$\frac{5}{8}$ ____ $\frac{7}{10}$ $-\frac{5}{6}$ ____ -5 $\frac{1}{2}$ ____ $-\frac{1}{2}$

$\frac{3}{4}$ ____ 0.8 $-\frac{2}{3}$ ____ 0 $-2\frac{1}{3}$ ____ -3

Fast Math

Solve.

$n + 1.5 = 2.7$ $n =$ _____ $m - 11.6 = 14.4$ $m =$ _____

$2.3 + 0.06 = b$ $b =$ _____ $\frac{y}{2.5} = 20$ $y =$ _____

$5.6t = 19.04$ $t =$ _____ $1.13 = r \div 0.09$ $r =$ _____

Think Tank

Pau's pool has an area of 615 square feet. It is $20\frac{1}{2}$ feet wide and $5\frac{1}{2}$ feet deep. The pool is rectangular. How much water will it hold if filled to the top?

_____

Show your work in the tank.

Data Place

The two graphs show dog-training DVD sales.

Use the data to answer the questions.

GRAPH A

GRAPH B

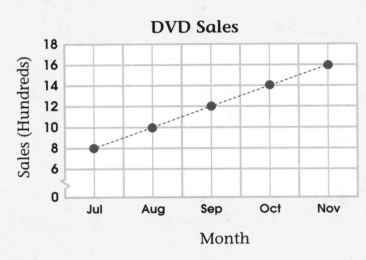

1. Do both graphs show the same data? _____

2. How do the graphs give a different impression of the data? _____

_____

3. Which graph gives the impression that
   sales are increasing more dramatically? _____

Puzzler

Here is a way to name 4. It uses fraction bars, a plus sign,
and the digits 1, 2, 3, 4, and 8 *once* each:

$$3\frac{1}{2} + \frac{4}{8} = 4$$

Now you try. Use fraction bars, a plus sign,
and the digits 1, 3, 4, 5, 6, and 8 *once* each to name 9.

Reading & Math Practice, Grade 6 © 2014 Scholastic Inc.

WORD of the Day

Use the word below in a short paragraph about a person bungling something.

inept: (adj.) *totally without skill or appropriateness; incompetent; clumsy*

_____

_____

_____

Sentence Mender

Rewrite the sentence to make it correct.

This morning I eight a egg wearing my pajamas

_____

Cursive Quote

Copy the quotation in cursive writing.

A book is the most effective weapon against intolerance and ignorance.

—Lyndon B. Johnson

_____

_____

_____

Do you agree? Explain. Write your answer in cursive on another sheet of paper.

Analogy of the Day

Complete the analogy.

Jovial is to **jolly** as _____ is to **steady**.

○ A. miserable   ○ B. constant   ○ C. changing   ○ D. immobile

Explain how the analogy works: _____

_____

📖 Ready, Set, READ!

Read the passage. Then answer the questions.

The word *bark*, meaning the sound a dog makes, comes from the Old English word *beorkan* and the Middle English word *berkin*. *Bark*, which names the tough exterior of a tree, comes from the Middle English word *borkr* and the Middle Low German word *borke*. But where does the expression *bark up the wrong tree* come from?

It goes back to colonial times. Many kinds of hunting dogs were called "coon dogs." Their job was to find raccoons. They chased them through the underbrush and then up into a tree. Once the dog had "treed" the raccoon, it would bark furiously at the base of that tree. This would alert the dog's master to come and shoot the trapped animal.

But the nocturnal raccoon was a crafty critter. It would often escape in the dark through the high branches to another tree. That left the hound below barking up the wrong tree.

1. Explain the everyday meaning of *barking up the wrong tree*. Give an example.

_____

_____

_____

_____

_____

_____

2. Which is the best title for this piece?
   - ○ A. Raccoon Hunting
   - ○ B. Two Kinds of Bark
   - ○ C. In the Nation's Capital
   - ○ D. Origin of an Idiom

🌀 BrainTeaser 🌀

What does each saying mean? Read the definitions on the right. Write the number on the line.

1. Don't **jump the gun**.	_____ being overly careful and tactful
2. Just **hold your tongue**.	_____ noisy but unproductive
3. Let's **shoot the breeze**.	_____ not totally healthy
4. We're **in the doghouse**.	_____ act too quickly
5. I got a **slap on the wrist**.	_____ being punished
6. He felt **under the weather**.	_____ chat casually
7. She's **walking on eggshells**.	_____ can't sit still
8. You're **all bark and no bite**.	_____ mild warning
9. They have **ants in their pants**.	_____ wait to speak

Number Place

Order the numbers from *least* to *greatest*.

1.6   1.2   −1.2   −1.6   _____

$\frac{1}{2}$ $-\frac{1}{2}$ $-1\frac{1}{2}$ 1   _____

10.1   −10.01   −10   10   _____

$2\frac{1}{4}$ −2 $-2\frac{1}{4}$ 2   _____

Fast Math

Solve.

$n + 1\frac{3}{5} = 3\frac{3}{10}$ $n =$ _____

$b - \frac{4}{7} = \frac{5}{14}$ $b =$ _____

$t - \frac{3}{5} = \frac{4}{5}$ $t =$ _____

$\frac{7}{9} - m = \frac{2}{9}$ $m =$ _____

$y = 2\frac{1}{4} + 5\frac{1}{8}$ $y =$ _____

$\frac{5}{8} + k = 3\frac{1}{8}$ $k =$ _____

Think Tank

Dina stacks 220 cans of soup at the store where she works. The top layer has 1 can. The next layer has 3 cans, the next has 6, then 10, and so on. How many layers are there?

_____

How many cans are in the bottom layer?

_____

Show your work in the tank.

Data Place

The stem-and-leaf plot shows the age at inauguration of 15 American presidents first inaugurated between 1923 and 2009.

Use the data to answer the questions below.

Age of 15 American Presidents at First Inauguration (1923–2009)	
Stem	Leaf
4	3 6 7
5	1 1 2 4 4 5 6
6	0 1 2 4 9

1. How many presidents were in their forties when they were inaugurated?

   _____

2. How many were 54 when inaugurated? _____

3. How old was the oldest of these presidents at inauguration? _____

4. What is the range of the ages of these presidents

   at their inaugurations? _____

5. What is the median age of these presidents at their inaugurations? _____

6. How many presidents were at least 55 when they were inaugurated? _____

Puzzler

Daniel is placing the DVDs he owns on a shelf. He has between 40 and 50 DVDs. He wants to place the same number on each shelf. If he uses 4 shelves, there are 3 left over. If he uses 6 shelves, 5 are left over.

How many DVDs does Daniel have? _____

WORD of the Day

Use the word below in a short paragraph about sabotage you have read about or have seen in a movie or on television.

sabotage: (n.) *an action taken to destroy something or to prevent something from working properly*

_____

_____

_____

Sentence Mender

Rewrite the sentence to make it correct.

My pals name is hard to spelling because her is from whales.

_____

Cursive Quote

Copy the quotation in cursive writing.

Develop a passion for learning. If you do, you will never cease to grow.

—Anthony J. D'Angelo

_____

_____

_____

Does this declaration make sense to you? Why? Write your view in cursive on another sheet of paper.

Analogy of the Day

Complete the analogy.

Sculptor is to **artist** as _____ is to **country**.

○ A. continent   ○ B. museum   ○ C. Peru   ○ D. city

Explain how the analogy works: _____

_____

Ready, Set, READ!

Read the memo. Then answer the questions.

Memo
To: Mom and Dad
From: Your loving and responsible children
Re: Caring for Huck

We know how busy you are and that you are seriously considering our request to get a puppy. Good! So we'll cut to the chase. Yes, Huck will be our dog's name. We will take full responsibility for Huck's care. We will love Huck so much.

Please read these points carefully.

• Dogs need routines. We'll keep Huck on a regular schedule:
  ✓ first walk at 7 A.M., followed by food
  ✓ second walk at lunchtime
  ✓ dinner at 5 P.M.; third walk follows

• Dogs need training. We will set aside half an hour each day to teach Huck these key commands: *sit, stay, come, down, wait, leave it, drop, no.*

• We will draw up and sign a contract that lists these obligations.

We await your thoughtful response. You know where to find us.

Sincerely,
Your very responsible son and daughter

1. What does *cut to the chase* mean?
   ○ A. Get out of here now!
   ○ B. Get to the point.
   ○ C. Get a new dog.
   ○ D. Run faster.

2. Why did the kids send a memo, not a text or e-mail?
   ○ A. To act mature and businesslike
   ○ B. To practice business writing
   ○ C. They don't have a smart phone.
   ○ D. They are in business school.

☉ BrainTeaser ☉

What is the largest ant in the world?

Solve each clue. Then copy each letter into its numbered box to find the answer to the riddle.

• Scientific word for skulls

  __9__ __5__ __4__ __2__ __8__ __1__

• Diplomacy

  __7__ __10__ __6__ __3__

1	2	3	4	5	6	7	8	9	10

Reading & Math Practice, Grade 6 © 2014 Scholastic Inc.

Number Place

Circle the numbers divisible by 5.

400   7,512   85   1,101   145,405

Circle the numbers divisible by 4.

234   92   164   9,462   65,408

Circle the numbers divisible by 6.

330   573   132   1,172   12,408

Fast Math

Solve.

$\frac{5}{8} n = 95$ $n =$ _____

$5b = 5\frac{5}{8}$ $b =$ _____

$\frac{8}{15} t = 1\frac{1}{9}$ $t =$ _____

$\frac{5}{8} m \div \frac{8}{9} = 21$ $m =$ _____

$w \div \frac{2}{3} = \frac{6}{7}$ $w =$ _____

$2p + \frac{1}{2} p = 25$ $p =$ _____

Think Tank

Six friends finish two-thirds of a job in one day. They share the work equally. What fraction of the day's work does each do?

_____

Show your work in the tank.

Data Place

Place the numbers 1, 2, 3, 6, 7, 8, 11, and 14 where they belong in the diagram.

Numbers less than 10   Numbers greater than 3

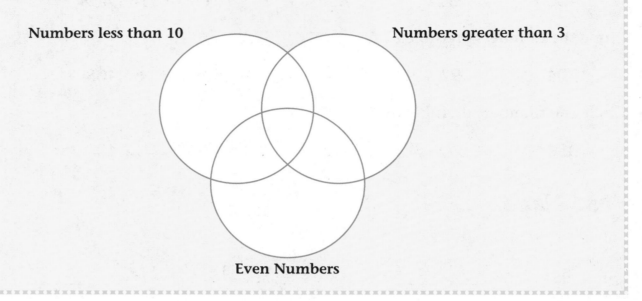

Even Numbers

Puzzler

The map shows where dinosaur bones have been found. The four paleontologists on the site want to divide the region so that each can examine the same number of bones. Show how this can be accomplished using only two straight lines.

Each • is a location of a bone.

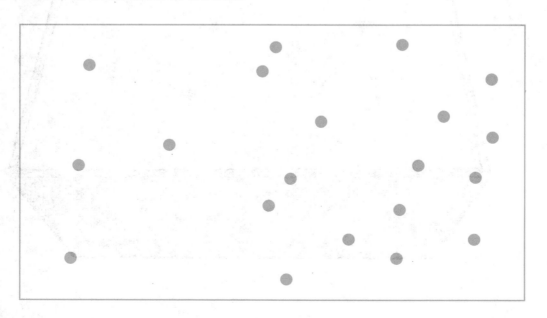

154

WORD of the Day

Use the word below in a short paragraph about a performance or achievement that earned a standing ovation.

ovation: (n.) *an enthusiastic public welcome; an outburst of applause or clapping*

_____

_____

_____

Sentence Mender

Rewrite the sentence to make it correct.

Please be keep this secret among the to of us.

_____

Cursive Quote

Copy the quotation in cursive writing.

You may be disappointed if you fail, but you are doomed if you don't try.

—Beverly Sills

_____

_____

_____

Do you agree? Explain. Write your answer in cursive on another sheet of paper.

Analogy of the Day

Complete the analogy.

Ballet is to **dance** as _____ is to **gemstone**.

○ A. jewelry   ○ B. necklace   ○ C. shiny   ○ D. ruby

Explain how the analogy works: _____

_____

📖 Ready, Set, READ!

Read the movie review. Then answer the questions.

Lost on the Moon, a movie review

Have you ever been on a giant, scary roller coaster? If you have, then you'll have a sense of what watching *Lost on the Moon* is like. Buy your ticket, find your seat, and then hold on tight.

The movie begins as Devin leaves the isolated base to take a walk with his faithful ferret, Fuzzy. But they take a wrong turn. Do they ever! Without giving anything away, I can tell you that Devin and Fuzzy have an adventure that would make Indiana Jones and Han Solo proud. They meet creatures you don't ever want to meet. (When that huge paw greets them at the bottom of that deep crevasse . . .) They face dangers King Kong would shy away from. Famous movie directors Ridley Scott, George Lucas, and Steven Spielberg would marvel at the special effects and amazing scenery. And the unexpected twists and turns in the plot would make a gymnast ache.

Go see this surefire blockbuster. It's a scream! Take along a calm friend.

1. What does the reviewer like about this movie? _____

_____

2. What technique does the reviewer use to support his or her views of aspects of the

movie? _____

_____

_____

3. How do you interpret the reviewer's last sentence? _____

_____

🌀 BrainTeaser 🌀

How many different words can you spell with letters
from the word *responsibilities*? Every word must have
at least three letters. List them here.

_____

_____

_____

_____

Reading & Math Practice, Grade 6 © 2014 Scholastic Inc.

Number Place

Write whether the number is divisible by 2, 3, 4, 5, 6, 8, 9, and/or 10.

333   8,410   67,704   90,990   352,860

_____   _____   _____   _____   _____

Fast Math

Add or subtract.

+3 + +2 = _____   +3 + −5 = _____   +6 − +2 = _____

+5 − −5 = _____   +7 − +7 = _____   −7 + −8 = _____

−2 − +2 = _____   −4 + +2 + −6 = _____   +3 + −2 + −5 = _____

Think Tank

Art is making 3 pennants in the shape of isosceles triangles. Each will have a $1\frac{3}{4}$ -foot base and will be $5\frac{1}{3}$ feet long. Find the total area of all 3 pennants.

_____

Show your work in the tank.

Data Place

Here are the numbers of points the school's basketball team scored in home games this season.

47 54 70 62 59 62 82 66 62 73 55 82 59

Make a stem-and-leaf plot for this set of data.
Find the range, median, and mode of the data.

1. Range _____   2. Median _____   3. Mode _____

4. Which measure best represents the data? _____

Puzzler

Choose any integer. Follow the 12 steps to see a number trick.

1. Add −15.   2. Subtract −13.   3. Add +19.

4. Subtract −9.   5. Subtract +4.   6. Subtract +17.

7. Add +8.   8. Subtract −12.   9. Add +11.

10. Subtract +2.   11. Subtract +16.   12. Add −18.

What do you notice? _____

Choose another integer and try the trick again.

Reading & Math Practice, Grade 6 © 2014 Scholastic Inc.

WORD of the Day

Use the word below in a short paragraph about something you know to be definitely true.

indisputable: (adj.) *beyond question or argument; definitely true*

_____

_____

_____

Sentence Mender

Rewrite the sentence to make it correct.

We have see amazeing fotos of Jupiters' moon's.

_____

Cursive Quote

Copy the quotation in cursive writing.

The present was an egg laid by the past that had the future inside its shell.

—Zora Neale Hurston

_____

_____

_____

What do you think Hurston meant by this? Write your answer in cursive on another sheet of paper.

Analogy of the Day

Complete the analogy.

Wood is to **hard** as _____ is to **hot**.

○ A. cold   ○ B. day   ○ C. fire   ○ D. soft

Explain how the analogy works: _____

_____

📖 Ready, Set, READ!

Read the passage. Then answer the questions.

How nice it is to take a long, relaxing bath. People have been enjoying bathing in tubs for many centuries. The ancient Greeks and Romans believed that doing so was a measure of how civilized they were.

Bathtubs were probably invented independently in different places, but we know that the Minoans of ancient Crete had them nearly 4,000 years ago. Their great palace at Knossos boasted bathrooms with elegant clay tubs and sunken floors. But they had no plumbing. The tubs had handles. They could be carried outside and emptied. In palaces built a little later on Crete, the bathrooms had sloped stone floors. Overflowing tubs in these would empty into gutters. The gutters were part of a sophisticated water system that used clay pipes.

The Cretans were so fond of bathing that their coffins looked exactly like their bathtubs. These coffins had lids. But they had plug holes, too.

1. Why was bathing so important to the Greeks and Romans?

   _____

   _____

2. In what important ways did bathrooms in ancient Crete differ from ours?

   _____

   _____

🗩 BrainTeaser 🗩

Solve the puzzle. It has a three-letter word on top and a nine-letter word at the bottom. Going down, each word uses the same letters as the word above it, plus one more, and then rearranged.

Clues:

• had lunch

• slash

• judges the worth of something

• looked at for a long time

• cooked a turkey

• open sporty automobile

• shared top billing

Reading & Math Practice, Grade 6 © 2014 Scholastic Inc.

Number Place

Is the number prime, composite, or neither? Write *p*, *c*, or *n*.

32 _____   19 _____   81 _____   41 _____   207 _____

Write True or False. Then explain your choice.

All prime numbers are odd numbers. _____

_____

The sum of two prime numbers is a composite number. _____

_____

Fast Math

Find the product.

+4 × +2 = _____   +8 × −5 = _____   +6 × +21 = _____

+50 × −5 = _____   0 × +7 = _____   −12 × −8 = _____

−2 × +20 = _____   −4 × +2 × −6 = _____   +3 × −2 × +7 = _____

Think Tank

The average daily temperature in Calgary for each of seven days was −2°C, −3°C, −1°C, +2°C, −2°C, +4°C and +1°C. What was the median temperature in Calgary that week?

_____

Show your work in the tank.

Data Place

Here are the scores Nora got on her social studies tests in this marking period.

63 90 52 90 56 73 61

Select from mean, median, or mode to answer the following questions. Then give the actual measure.

1. What measure of average should Nora's teacher use to describe her scores

   most accurately? _____

2. What measure should Nora use to show her scores in the best light?

   _____

3. What measure would describe Nora's scores the least favorably? _____

   _____

Puzzler

Write *Yes* or *No* to answer each question. If *No*, explain why.

1. Can you make a triangle that has

   two obtuse angles? _____

2. Can you make a quadrilateral that has

   no right angles? _____

3. Can you make a pentagon that has

   four obtuse angles? _____

4. Can you make a parallelogram that has

   four congruent acute angles? _____

WORD of the Day

Use the word below in a short paragraph about a person dealing with bad news or a challenge.

cope: (v.) *struggle successfully against; deal with satisfactorily; manage; get along*

_____

_____

_____

Sentence Mender

Rewrite the sentence to make it correct.

"Yes we went to the famous zoo when we visit san diego, said Lis aunt."

_____

Cursive Quote

Copy the quotation in cursive writing.

Our greatest glory is not in never failing, but in rising up every time we fail.

—Ralph Waldo Emerson

_____

_____

_____

Does this idea make sense? Explain. Write your answer in cursive on another sheet of paper

Analogy of the Day

Complete the analogy.

Menacing is to **benign** as _____ is to **maximum**.

○ A. ominous   ○ B. reassuring   ○ C. most   ○ D. minimum

Explain how the analogy works: _____

_____

📖 Ready, Set, READ!

Read the lyrics. Then answer the questions.

Here is the first verse and chorus of "Home on the Range."

Oh, give me a home, where the buffalo roam,
Where the deer and the antelope play,
Where seldom is heard a discouraging word,
And the skies are not cloudy all day.

Chorus:
Home, home on the range,
Where the deer and the antelope play,
Where seldom is heard a discouraging word,
And the skies are not cloudy all day.

Here are two more verses in this famous folksong.

Where the air is so pure, the zephyrs so free,
The breezes so balmy and light,
That I would not exchange my home on the range
For all the cities so bright.

How often at night when the heavens are bright
With the light of the glittering stars,
Have I stood here amazed and asked as I gazed
If their glory exceeds that of ours.

1. What does the songwriter like about living on the open range?

_____

_____

2. What does the songwriter think when he looks up at the stars?

_____

_____

🌀 BrainTeaser 🌀

The word bank lists mythological character names. Each one is hidden in the puzzle. Find and circle each name.

Word Bank

ACHILLES	CALLIOPE	HERCULES
ADONIS	CIRCE	ICARUS
AJAX	CUPID	LEDA
APOLLO	DEMETER	MEDUSA
ATHENA	DIANA	MIDAS
AURORA	ELECTRA	ORPHEUS

```
Y D D I P U C M I D A S A
O O R P H E U S X A J A R
S E L U C R E H Z M K A O
Z S E L L I H C A Q I M R
V F G D E M E T E R C E U
S I N O D A L E D A A D A
A E P O I L L A C F R U N
O E L E C T R A J P U S J
A N A I D E C R I C S A Z
O L L O P A A N E H T A I
```

Reading & Math Practice, Grade 6 © 2014 Scholastic Inc.

Number Place

Write the absolute value of each number.

−326 _____   −15 _____   18 _____   −4.5 _____ $-\frac{2}{5}$ _____

−0.6 _____   −22 _____   0 _____   −87 _____ $-\frac{5}{8}$ _____

Fast Math

Add or subtract. Write your answer in simplest form.

$+3\frac{1}{2} + {+2} =$ _____ $+2 + {-\frac{5}{8}} =$ _____ $+6 - {+\frac{2}{3}} =$ _____

$+\frac{5}{8} - {-\frac{5}{8}} =$ _____ $+\frac{7}{20} - {+\frac{7}{20}} =$ _____ $-0.5 + {-8.5} =$ _____

$$\begin{array}{r} -2.2 \\ - \ +2.5 \\ \hline \end{array}$$
$$\begin{array}{r} -\frac{4}{5} \\ + \ +\frac{2}{5} \\ \hline \end{array}$$
$$\begin{array}{r} +\frac{3}{4} \\ + \ -\frac{2}{3} \\ \hline \end{array}$$

Think Tank

Five painters can paint 5 houses in 5 days. How many days will it take 2 painters to paint 1 house?

_____

Show your work in the tank.

Reading & Math Practice, Grade 6 © 2014 Scholastic Inc.

Data Place

Complete the function table for the function $y = x + 0.5$.

Then draw the graph of the function on the coordinate grid.

x	x + 0.5	(x, y)
0		
1		
2		

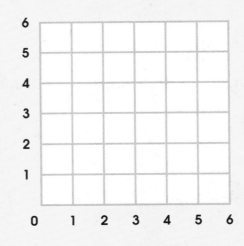

1. Is $y = x + 0.5$ a linear function? _____

2. How do you know? _____

Puzzler

Each clock is a mirror reflection.

Tell the actual time for each.

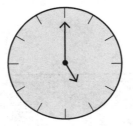      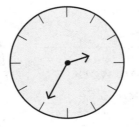

_____   _____   _____

Reading & Math Practice, Grade 6 © 2014 Scholastic Inc.

WORD of the Day

Use the word below in a short paragraph about a person who is an individualist.

nonconformist: (n.) *a person who refuses to be bound by established customs or ways of doing things*

_____

_____

_____

Sentence Mender

Rewrite the sentence to make it correct.

My friend and me saw a collection of thirty seven fossles at an museum.

_____

Cursive Quote

Copy the quotation in cursive writing.

If you have much, give of your wealth; if you have little, give of your heart.

—Arabic proverb

_____

_____

_____

What do you think about this proverb? Write your answer in cursive on another sheet of paper.

Analogy of the Day

Complete the analogy.

Protractor is to **measure** as _____ is to **dig**.

○ A. spade   ○ B. hole   ○ C. compass   ○ D. dirt

Explain how the analogy works: _____

_____

📖 Ready, Set, READ!

Read the passage. Then answer the questions.

For some people, life is not easy. They face many challenges but obtain few pleasures. In their eyes, things rarely work out as they'd like them to. They have little faith in the goodness of others. These people might conclude that life is "not a bed of roses."

This expression for a pessimistic view of life goes back to Charles Dickens, who wrote the following in *Oliver Twist*: "A parochial life is not a bed of roses." But the idiom's roots go further back. It was in the 17th century when something desirable was first compared to a bed of soft, silky petals.

For other people, life generally looks brighter. They believe that things will work out because they regard others as basically good and decent. For these optimists, "life is a bowl of cherries." This expression arrived much later—in the 1920s. It was common slang that meant that life is sweet.

1. What's your view: Is life a *bowl of cherries* or *not a bed of roses*? Explain.

_____

_____

2. Summarize the contrasting views of *optimists* and *pessimists*.

_____

_____

🌀 BrainTeaser 🌀

Each word below has two pairs of double letters. All missing pairs appear in the letter bank. Some words use two different pairs, while others use two of the same pair. Fill in the missing pairs to complete each word.

Letter Bank

cc ee ll
nn rr ss
tt zz

1. vo ☐☐ eyba ☐☐

2. emba ☐☐ a ☐☐

3. wh ☐☐ lba ☐☐ ow

4. pe ☐☐ ile ☐☐

5. fu ☐☐ ba ☐☐ s

6. bu ☐☐ an ☐☐ r

7. ca ☐☐ e ☐☐ e

8. o ☐☐ u ☐☐ ed

Reading & Math Practice, Grade 6 © 2014 Scholastic Inc.

Number Place

Express each using exponents. Then write the product.

$2 \times 2 \times 2$ _____ $2 \times 2 \times 3 \times 3 \times 3$ _____

$3 \times 3 \times 3 \times 3 \times 4$ _____ $5 \times 12 \times 5 \times 5$ _____

$3 \times 3 \times 4 \times 4 \times 4$ _____ $6 \times 2 \times 6 \times 2$ _____

Fast Math

Replace the variable with an integer to make the inequality true.

$n > 9$ _____ $m < -21$ _____

$b < -5$ _____ $y \leq -1$ _____

$n + 3 > 5$ _____ $r + 2 \leq -2$ _____

Think Tank

A baseball game being played in Seattle is televised in Baltimore, where Wanda is watching it. The game began at 8:05 P.M. in Seattle and lasted for $2\frac{3}{4}$ hours. Wanda turned off the game as soon as it ended. What time did she turn off the television?

_____

Show your work in the tank.

Data Place

The scatter plot shows temperatures one evening.

Use the data to answer the questions.

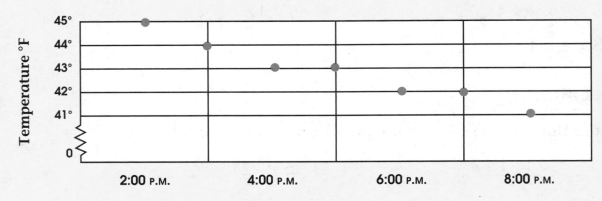

Time of Day

1. What correlation, if any, is there between temperature and time? Explain.

   _____

2. Over what period of time was the temperature at or below 43°F? _____

Puzzler

Phan's property is in the shape of a square, with 100 meters on a side. His neighbor has a hungry goat so Phan wants to fence in the property. The fence will have a post every 10 meters. How many posts will the fence have?

_____

Draw a sketch to help you figure it out.

WORD of the Day

Use the word below in a short paragraph about a jolly fictional person.

jovial: (adj.) *good humored; merry; jolly*

_____

_____

_____

Sentence Mender

Rewrite the sentence to make it correct.

I buy me a round trip-ticket on the three oclock train to Santafe New mexico.

_____

Cursive Quote

Copy the quotation in cursive writing.

Yesterday is ashes; tomorrow wood. Only today does the fire burn brightly.
         —Inuit proverb

_____

_____

_____

Explain what this proverb means. Write your answer in cursive on another sheet of paper.

Analogy of the Day

Complete the analogy.

Putter is to **golfer** as _____ is to **electrician**.

○ A. driver   ○ B. wire   ○ C. electricity   ○ D. telephone

Explain how the analogy works: _____

_____

📖 Ready, Set, READ!

Read the passage. Then answer the questions.

Do you like bananas in your cereal? Do you enjoy banana ice cream, banana yogurt, or banana pudding? How about a slice of banana bread or banana cream pie? Have you ever slipped on a banana peel?

The banana has been a world traveler. It had its beginnings in Malaysia. By the sixth century BCE, it had made its way to India, where Alexander the Great tasted it in 327 BCE. By the third century, bananas were being cultivated in southern China.

Eventually, the banana arrived in Madagascar, an island off the southeastern coast of Africa. Arab traders found it there and brought it with them to West Africa, where it got the attention of the Portuguese. They, in turn, planted it in their Canary Islands. Then, in the early 16th century, explorers brought the banana with them to the Caribbean, where it became a very popular food. It was only finger-sized then. In fact, the name banana comes from the Arabic word *banan*, which means finger.

It took another 350 years for bananas to come to America. They made their appearance at a centennial celebration in Pennsylvania. There they were wrapped in tin foil and sold for a dime to intrigued customers. But it wasn't until after World War I, when refrigeration was first installed in ocean-going ships, that bananas became readily available to Americans.

The banana plant, by the way, is not a tree. It is the world's largest herb.

1. Why did it take so long for bananas to become readily available in the United States?

_____

_____

2. What supports the author's claim that "the banana has been a world traveler"?

_____

_____

🌀 BrainTeaser 🌀

Solve these puzzling riddles. Each has a logical answer, but you'll have to think hard to figure it out.

1. How far can a wolf run into the woods?

_____

2. Name three consecutive days *without* using Sunday, Monday, Tuesday, Wednesday, Thursday, Friday, or Saturday. _____

3. What's black when you buy it, red when you use it, and gray when you discard it?

_____

Reading & Math Practice, Grade 6 © 2014 Scholastic Inc.

Number Place

Compare. Write **<**, **=**, or **>**.

2^3 ____ 3^2 $\qquad$ 2^5 ____ 2×5 $\qquad$ 4^3 ____ 64

5^3 ____ 2^6 $\qquad$ 3^4 ____ $2^3 \times 3^2$ $\qquad$ 6^3 ____ $2 \times 5 \times 5 \times 5$

2^2 ____ $(0.2)^2$ $\qquad$ $(\frac{1}{2})^3$ ____ $(\frac{1}{4})^3$ $\qquad$ $(0.6)^3$ ____ $(\frac{1}{2})^2$

Fast Math

Write each ratio in simplest form.

4 to 12 $\qquad$ 8 : 20 $\qquad$ $\frac{21}{63}$ $\qquad$ 12 to 18 $\qquad$ 50 : 30

____ $\qquad$ ____ $\qquad$ ____ $\qquad$ ____ $\qquad$ ____

24 to 12 $\qquad$ 14 : 3.5 $\qquad$ $\frac{12}{84}$ $\qquad$ 1.2 to 2.0 $\qquad$ 5 : 2.5

____ $\qquad$ ____ $\qquad$ ____ $\qquad$ ____ $\qquad$ ____

 Think Tank

What is the ratio
of infielders to outfielders?

_____

What is the ratio
of infielders to players?

_____

**Show your work
in the tank.**

Players on a Baseball Team

3 outfielders

4 infielders

1 catcher

1 pitcher

Think Tank

Data Place

This quilt is made of 25 square sections sewn together. The quilt represents one whole.

What percent is represented by

1. the dotted sections? _____

2. the starred sections? _____

3. the dotted, starred, and circle sections?

   _____

4. all the sections? _____

5. all but the sections with crossed lines? _____

6. 1 quilt plus all the dotted and circle sections? _____

Puzzler

Make one straight cut in this figure so that the two pieces you form can be reassembled into a square.
Draw a dotted line to show where to cut.

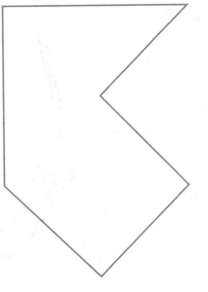

Reading & Math Practice, Grade 6 © 2014 Scholastic Inc.

WORD of the Day

Use the word below in a short paragraph about a fire.

douse: (v.) *plunge into a liquid; put out quickly; drench; immerse*

_____

_____

_____

Sentence Mender

Rewrite the sentence to make it correct.

Galileo was a scientist who's ideas was not excepted during when he lived.

_____

Cursive Quote

Copy the quotation in cursive writing.

Wise sayings often fall on barren ground but a kind word is never thrown away.

—Arthur Helps

_____

_____

_____

Do you agree? Explain. Write your answer in cursive on another sheet of paper.

Analogy of the Day

Complete the analogy.

Mezzanine is to **stadium** as _____ is to **city**.

○ A. mountain ○ B. county ○ C. skyscraper ○ D. roof

Explain how the analogy works: _____

_____

Ready, Set, READ!

Read the story. Then answer the questions.

There are three cloth napkins on our dining table. In the kitchen, two dish towels hang from cabinet knobs. To the right of our front door there is a large, heavy mat. My dog has found a use for all of these things.

When she comes in, she lies down on the mat to await instructions. She's been trained to do this. When someone comes to our door with a delivery, we open the door and she comes to inspect. Then she trots over to the table and snatches a napkin. She'll parade around with it for a moment and then gift it to her "guest." She'll do this every time.

When someone visits that she knows, even a little, the napkin simply isn't good enough. She prances into the kitchen, retrieves a towel, parades it about, and then offers it to her friend. She does this every time, too.

But when we come back home, whether away for ten minutes or ten hours, she goes whole hog in her response. No mere napkin or dish towel will do. She hoists up her large mat, scampers about with it, then leaps on the bed, mat in mouth, and deposits it there. And there she waits for us, proudly wagging her tail in delight.

1. How does the dog decide which gift to give?

_____

_____

2. What does it mean to *go whole hog*?

_____

_____

☺ BrainTeaser ☺

Use logic to match each person with a room and a game.
Use the grid to keep track of what you figure out.

- The study computer was not used for pinball.

- Ted was playing Neopets, but not in the den.

- Neither Paco nor Ted was in the kitchen.

- Kita wasn't playing Tetris, but Paco was.

Name	Room	Game
Kita		
Paco		
Ted		

Reading & Math Practice, Grade 6 © 2014 Scholastic Inc.

Number Place

Find the prime factorization. Write it in exponential form.

8 _____   32 _____   125 _____

50 _____   60 _____   96 _____

Fast Math

Circle each ratio equivalent to the first ratio.

3 : 2	30 to 2	9 to 6	$\frac{15}{9}$	36 : 24
$\frac{10}{7}$	20 : 14	25 to 14	1 to 0.7	$\frac{1}{7}$
45 to 25	50 : 30	9 to 5	5 to 9	$\frac{40}{20}$

Which ratios are equivalent? Write = or ≠.

$\frac{7}{8}$ ___ 16 to 14 $\frac{5}{12}$ ___ 15 : 36   10 : 4 ___ $\frac{25}{10}$

$\frac{2}{5}$ ___ 10 to 4 $\frac{36}{48}$ ___ 3 : 4   1.5 : 0.5 ___ $\frac{3}{1}$

💡 Think Tank

Becca plays on a basketball team. She has 3 uniform tops, 2 pairs of shorts, and 2 pairs of sneakers. How many different outfits can she put together if she always wears a top, shorts, and sneakers when she plays?

_____

Show your work in the tank.

Data Place

Fiona opens a grocery in a town that already has two. She wants to offer the lowest prices. To do this, she figures out which of her competitors has the lowest unit prices for what she sells. She then make her unit price 2¢ less. But, Fiona sells her products only in packages of 5!

Complete the table to find Fiona's price for five of the items shown.

Item	Gil's Grocery	Mira's Market	Fiona's Foods
Corn Muffin	4 for $6	10 for $18	5 for
Yogurt	4 for $3.40	6 for $4.62	5 for
Canned Tuna	6 for $7.50	4 for $4.88	5 for

Puzzler

For each object, draw the *top* view, *front* view, and *side* view.

Object	Top View	Front View	Side View

WORD of the Day

Use the word below in a short paragraph about a precious memento or souvenir you cherish.

keepsake: (n.) *something kept in memory of the giver; memento; souvenir*

_____

_____

_____

Sentence Mender

Rewrite the sentence to make it correct.

John Woo the Director have a film showing at the Festival next Year.

_____

Cursive Quote

Copy the quotation in cursive writing.

A fool finds no pleasure in understanding but delights in airing his own opinions.

—Turkish proverb

_____

_____

_____

Describe someone who is a "fool" like this. Write your description in cursive on another sheet of paper.

Analogy of the Day

Complete the analogy.

Straw is to **drink** as _____ is to **clean**.

○ A. room   ○ B. mop   ○ C. dish   ○ D. paint

Explain how the analogy works: _____

_____

Reading & Math Practice, Grade 6 © 2014 Scholastic Inc.

📖 Ready, Set, READ!

Read the passage. Then answer the questions.

How would you like an adventure in a national park like no other? There's one that has no majestic mountains, no deep canyons or colorful rock formations, no waterfalls, caves, or pine trees. There are no moose and no bear. There's also no way to get to Dry Tortugas National Park by car.

Dry Tortugas consists of a cluster of small islands about 70 miles west of Key West, Florida. You can reach it only by boat or seaplane. It is home not to buffalo or elk, but to lush sea grass and beautiful coral reefs that throb with life. Green sea turtles and migratory birds like sooty terns, frigate birds, and brown noddies also reside there. The park is so remote that your cell phone won't work. It is so dry that you have to bring along your own water. In fact, you'll have to bring food and everything else you'll need because the park has no stores.

Among the things to bring are bathing suits, snorkeling or diving gear, sunscreen and binoculars. You'll want to check out the reefs and the nearly 300 shipwrecks. And history buffs will want to explore the well-preserved Fort Jefferson. It was built in the 19th century with 16 million bricks. Don't miss a visit to this unique park!

1. Which are you likely to find on Dry Tortugas National Park?
   - ○ A. bison
   - ○ B. ski slopes
   - ○ C. cafeterias
   - ○ D. water birds

2. What distinguishes Dry Tortugas from most other national parks?
   - ○ A. It is beautiful.
   - ○ B. It has no large mammals.
   - ○ C. It cannot be reached by car.
   - ○ D. It is private land.

⚙ BrainTeaser ⚙

The starting letters in all the two-word phrases below are missing. The remaining letters, while *in order*, are pushed together. Both words in the phrase start with the same letter. Decide which letter is missing from each two-word phrase, then rewrite the phrase. The first one is done for you.

1. a s t e r i n d ___mastermind___

2. a b y o t t l e _____

3. o o k i e u t t e r _____

4. r e a k y r i d a y _____

5. e l p i n g a n d s _____

6. r e e n i a n t _____

7. i m e r a v e l _____

8. e c r e t e r v i c e _____

9. u t o r n e r s _____

10. i g h t u r s e _____

Reading & Math Practice, Grade 6 © 2014 Scholastic Inc.

Number Place

Write two equivalent fractions or mixed numbers for each.

$\frac{1}{2}$ _____

$\frac{3}{5}$ _____

$-\frac{3}{8}$ _____

$1\frac{1}{2}$ _____

$-3\frac{2}{5}$ _____

$5\frac{3}{10}$ _____

$-\frac{1}{4}$ _____

$-\frac{2}{7}$ _____

$-3\frac{7}{8}$ _____

Fast Math

Find the unit rate or unit price.

28 miles in 4 hours _____

6 DVDs for $42 _____

96 feet in 12 seconds _____

6 cards for $21 _____

24 pages read in 16 minutes _____

1 dozen cans for $7.20 _____

Think Tank

A bottle has a capacity of 1.8 L. Two-thirds of it holds eye care solution. If each dose is 2 mL, how many doses are in the bottle?

_____

Show your work in the tank.

Data Place

Here are won-lost records of the top five pitchers in Big Mesa Little League history. Remarkably, all these stars had the same ratio of wins to losses.

Complete the table. Then answer the question.

Player	Years	Won	Lost
Lefty Lebowitz	1988–1990	42	14
Hands Hansen	1997–1999		16
Stringbean Gomez	2004–2006	36	
Baby Face Jonas	2008–2010		11
Big Mo Tanaka	2012–	15	

Legendary great Ted "Kid" Toomer won 57 games in the 1970s. What is the greatest number of games Kid could have lost and still have had a better record than any pitcher in the table? _____

Puzzler

A dot cube has these faces:

Draw the face opposite.

Draw the face opposite.

Reading & Math Practice, Grade 6 © 2014 Scholastic Inc.

WORD of the Day

Use the word below in a short paragraph about something that is impossible to count or foretell.

incalculable: (adj.) *too great to be counted; impossible to foretell; unpredictable; innumerable*

_____

_____

_____

Sentence Mender

Rewrite the sentence to make it correct.

Those Roses was the prettier flowers Ive ever scene?

_____

Cursive Quote

Copy the quotation in cursive writing.

What the people want is very simple. They want an America as good as its promise.

—Barbara Jordan

- -

- -

- -

What is that promise? Write your view in cursive on another sheet of paper.

Analogy of the Day

Complete the analogy.

Retrieve is to **recover** as _____ is to **irritate**.

○ A. gladden   ○ B. scratch   ○ C. delight   ○ D. irk

Explain how the analogy works: _____

_____

📖 Ready, Set, READ!

Read the passage. Then answer the questions.

About 2,300 years ago, the patriotic Chinese poet Qu Yuan drowned himself. The traditional Chinese holiday of *Duan Yang*, or the Dragon Boat Festival, commemorates that event every year on the fifth day of the fifth lunar month. This usually falls sometime in June.

According to legend, when the poet drowned, villagers threw rice dumplings wrapped in bamboo leaves into the river. Their plan was to provide the fish with food to eat so they would leave the famous poet alone. Rice dumplings are still made and eaten during the festival. It is also said that people paddled out in their dragon boats to retrieve the body or to scare away the fish. That paddling is the origin of dragon boat racing.

Dragon boats are long, narrow rowing boats that are brightly painted. Each is adorned with a dragon's head at its prow. Men from neighboring villages row the boats, matching the rhythms of beating drums. In the evening, the boats parade along the water, festooned with colorful lanterns.

The Dragon Boat Festival is celebrated in other Asian countries besides China. A spectacular international version takes place every year in the Hong Kong harbor. Some American cities with large Asian populations also celebrate the day.

1. Why did the villagers row out into the river where Qu Yuan drowned?

_____

_____

2. What does *festooned* mean? _____

_____

🌀 BrainTeaser 🌀

Use the clues to fill in the grid with five different words. The word that goes in the first row also goes in the first column. The word that goes in the second row also goes in the second column, and so on. Choose their order carefully.

Clues:

• glowing coal or ash _____

• sticky substance from trees _____

• muscle that pumps blood _____

• style; move in one direction _____

• treat cruelly or harshly _____

Number Place

Rename in simplest form.

$\frac{12}{24}$ _____ $\frac{16}{20}$ _____ $\frac{3}{18}$ _____ $-\frac{16}{28}$ _____ $-\frac{20}{32}$ _____

$-\frac{6}{27}$ _____ $-\frac{9}{45}$ _____ $1\frac{6}{8}$ _____ $1\frac{6}{15}$ _____ $-2\frac{14}{18}$ _____

Fast Math

Do the ratios form a proportion? Write yes or no.

$\frac{2}{3} \overset{?}{=} \frac{6}{9}$ _____ $\frac{2}{5} \overset{?}{=} \frac{6}{20}$ _____ $\frac{7}{2} \overset{?}{=} \frac{14}{5}$ _____

$\frac{2}{7} \overset{?}{=} \frac{6}{24}$ _____ $\frac{2}{8} \overset{?}{=} \frac{8}{32}$ _____ $\frac{1}{3} \overset{?}{=} \frac{6}{18}$ _____

$\frac{12}{30} \overset{?}{=} \frac{6}{60}$ _____ $\frac{8}{3} \overset{?}{=} \frac{40}{9}$ _____ $\frac{81}{3} \overset{?}{=} \frac{27}{1}$ _____

Think Tank

A rectangular rug measures 35 feet by 28 feet. How many feet must be cut from both its length and width so that the ratio of the shorter side to the longer side is 3 to 4?

_____

Show your work in the tank.

Data Place

Seven cards have geometric figures on them.
What could each ratio represent?

1. $\frac{1}{2}$ _____

2. $\frac{2}{7}$ _____

3. $\frac{1}{6}$ _____

4. $\frac{3}{1}$ _____

5. $\frac{2}{3}$ _____

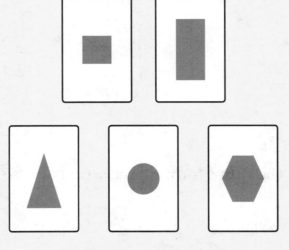

Puzzler

Draw three squares to separate each ✺ from every other ✺.

Hint: Think "inside the box."

186

WORD of the Day

Use the word below in a short paragraph about carefully forming an opinion, framing a law, or making a rule.

formulate: (v.) *express definitely or systematically; devise, invent*

_____

_____

_____

Sentence Mender

Rewrite the sentence to make it correct.

We sit around the kitchen's table and spoke about dads exciting news.

_____

Cursive Quote

Copy the quotation in cursive writing.

The woods would be very silent if no birds sang there except those that sang best.

—Henry Van Dyke

_____

_____

_____

What did Van Dyke mean by this? Write your answer in cursive on another sheet of paper.

Analogy of the Day

Complete the analogy.

Earring is to **jewelry** as _____ is to **planet**.

○ A. orbit   ○ B. moon   ○ C. sun   ○ D. Mars

Explain how the analogy works: _____

_____

📖 Ready, Set, READ!

Read the letter to the editor. Then answer the questions.

Dear Editor,

I am in the sixth grade. I read with interest your paper's editorial in support of coed classes. My classroom is coed; there are 15 girls and 13 boys. Although I know that some of my friends would disagree, I think that boys and girls should be in separate classes.

If we had classes without boys, the improvements would be noticeable right away. There would be no disruptive boys fighting, showing off, or teasing. Girls would be less likely to fear showing how smart they are. They would ask and answer questions more comfortably. Academics would rule. And some subjects, like personal hygiene and sex education, would be easier to discuss thoughtfully and openly without boys around. I'd guess that most boys would agree with this.

I know that men and women do many things together in life, from raising families to running corporations to playing on the same sports teams. We do need coed experiences. But we don't need them in our classrooms. When boys and girls are together in school, there are too many distractions. It's hard to focus on learning. There are plenty of opportunities for middle school boys and girls to interact outside the classroom.

Thank you,
Sangheeta Patel

1. How would you summarize Sangheeta's argument?

_____

_____

2. Would you say that Sangheeta's views are based in fact or opinion? Explain.

_____

_____

🌀 BrainTeaser 🌀

Find and cross out the extra word in each sentence below.

1. They say that the best things in life line are free.

2. Do you think tank I might borrow your class notes?

3. You can't possibly make believe that ridiculous excuse!

4. The new bike bill rack was installed in a convenient location.

5. Which of these drawers is the one that holds on the graph paper?

Number Place

Express each fraction as a mixed number in simplest form.

$\frac{12}{7}$ _____ $\frac{16}{6}$ _____ $-\frac{32}{12}$ _____ $\frac{36}{8}$ _____ $-\frac{20}{12}$ _____

Express each mixed number as a fraction in simplest form.

$-1\frac{2}{8}$ _____ $3\frac{7}{20}$ _____ $2\frac{8}{18}$ _____ $6\frac{5}{15}$ _____ $-2\frac{9}{39}$ _____

Fast Math

Find the value of n in each proportion.

$\frac{2}{5} = \frac{6}{n}$ _____ $\frac{n}{7} = \frac{6}{14}$ _____ $\frac{1}{n} = \frac{4}{52}$ _____

$\frac{n}{8} = \frac{6}{24}$ _____ $\frac{8}{5} = \frac{n}{35}$ _____ $\frac{5}{3} = \frac{n}{18}$ _____

$\frac{12}{20} = \frac{n}{60}$ _____ $\frac{n}{3} = \frac{42}{9}$ _____ $\frac{72}{9} = \frac{24}{n}$ _____

Think Tank

A cube has the same volume in cubic inches as its surface area in square inches. What is the length of one of the edges of the cube?

_____

Show your work in the tank.

Data Place

Wilson has a part-time job. The double line graph shows his monthly income and expenses for 6 months.

Use the data to answer the questions.

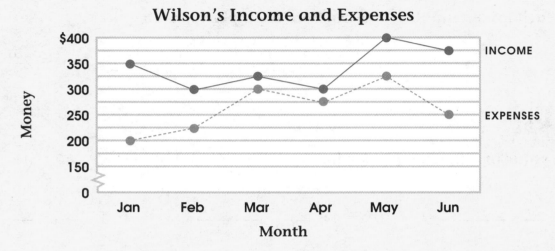

1. What was the difference between Wilson's income and expenses in May? _____

2. In which month did Wilson save the most money? _____

3. To the nearest dollar, what was the mean monthly difference between Wilson's income and his expenses? _____

4. In which month were Wilson's expenses the greatest percent of his income?

    _____

Puzzler

For each object, draw the *top* view, *front* view, and *side* view.

Object	Top View	Front View	Side View

Reading & Math Practice, Grade 6 © 2014 Scholastic Inc.

WORD of the Day

Use the word below in a short paragraph about a time you showed some initiative.

initiative: (n.) *the taking of the first step or move; the ability to act without being directed or urged*

_____

_____

_____

Sentence Mender

Rewrite the sentence to make it correct.

All my Buddy's shown up for my party last knight.

_____

Cursive Quote

Copy the quotation in cursive writing.

Outside of a dog, a book is man's best friend. Inside of a dog, it's too dark to read.

—Groucho Marx

- -

- -

- -

What does "outside of" mean, and what makes this quote funny? Write your answer in cursive on another sheet of paper.

Analogy of the Day

Complete the analogy.

Japan is to **Asia** as _____ is to **forest**.

○ A. tree   ○ B. mountain   ○ C. island   ○ D. continent

Explain how the analogy works: _____

_____

Ready, Set, READ!

Read the passage. Then answer the questions.

The Great Plains, where Febold Feboldson lived, get some weird weather. Take the year of the Great Fog that followed the year of the Great Heat that killed Paul Bunyan's blue ox.

The year began with 40 days of constant rain. But none of it reached the ground. It turned to steam, then cooled enough to become fog. The whole region was fogbound. The fog was so thick that people walked around in pairs—one to hold the fog back while the other passed through. The ranchers were delighted because their cattle could simply drink the fog. But the farmers were hopping mad because the sun couldn't shine through that dense fog. Their planted seeds didn't know which way was up. They grew downward.

Things for farmers got worse. They wanted to leave. That's when Febold came to the rescue. He cleverly thought to import an English fog cutter from London. Unfortunately, it didn't arrive until Thanksgiving, when the fog had turned to slush. This didn't stop Febold. He cut the slush into long strips and laid the strips atop the roads so as not to ruin the fields. The farmers stayed and their seeds began to get it right.

But ever since, many a rural traveler has cursed Febold and his fog cutter. That's because every spring when things thaw or it rains, the fog re-emerges to turn the country roads into impassible rivers.

1. What kind of story is this?
   - A. Meteorology report
   - B. Historical fiction
   - C. Tall tale
   - D. Myth

2. A good title for a movie of this tale might be
   - A. Slushy Roads
   - B. Fogbuster!
   - C. Feeble Febold
   - D. The Killing Heat

◉ BrainTeaser ◉

Write the missing word for each three-word expression.

1. pull your _____

2. pride and _____

3. push the _____

4. second to _____

5. take for _____

6. _____ your word

7. _____ and blood

8. _____ to say

9. _____ is money

10. _____ it quits

192

Number Place

Write each fraction as a decimal. Write each decimal as a fraction or mixed number in simplest form.

$-\frac{7}{10}$ _____

-0.06 _____

0.040 _____

$-\frac{3}{100}$ _____

$-7\frac{4}{5}$ _____

-44.55 _____

-0.014 _____

$61\frac{1}{8}$ _____

Fast Math

Write each percent as a fraction or mixed number in simplest form.

70% _____   5% _____   64% _____   150% _____

95% _____   225% _____   12% _____   124% _____

Write each fraction as a percent.

$\frac{2}{5}$ _____ $\frac{7}{8}$ _____ $\frac{24}{30}$ _____ $\frac{5}{8}$ _____

$\frac{8}{5}$ _____ $\frac{1}{25}$ _____ $\frac{7}{100}$ _____ $\frac{5}{4}$ _____

Think Tank

Two trapezoids are similar. The longer bases are 12 cm and 18 cm. If the length of the shorter base of the smaller trapezoid is 4 cm, how long is the shorter base of the larger trapezoid?

_____

Show your work in the tank.

Data Place

The circle graph shows the favorite kinds of TV programs the kids in Ms. Couch's class watch.

Use the data to answer the questions.

What percent of the students chose the following?

1. comedy _____

2. game show _____

3. sports or reality _____

4. drama or talk show _____

What percent did not choose the following?

5. comedy or sports _____

6. game show or drama _____

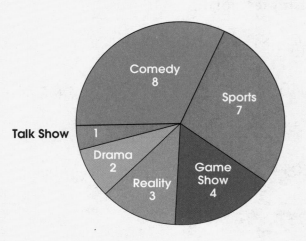

Favorite Kinds of TV Shows

Puzzler

Make a sketch to help you solve this problem.

Coach Koch arranges her basketball team in a circle. Her 12 players are evenly spaced around it. Each player passes the ball to the player directly opposite. The players are wearing uniforms numbered 1–12, and are standing in number order.
Who passes the ball to player 7?

_____

194

WORD of the Day

Use the word below in a short paragraph about someone or something that is either sure-footed or clever.

nimble: (adj.) *quick and skillful in movement; sure-footed; agile; clever*

_____

_____

_____

Sentence Mender

Rewrite the sentence to make it correct.

Isnt Carla more older than she brothers friend.

_____

Cursive Quote

Copy the quotation in cursive writing.

If you cannot find happiness along the road, you will not find it at the end of the road.
—Author unknown

_____

_____

What does this observation mean? Explain. Write your answer in cursive on another sheet of paper.

Analogy of the Day

Complete the analogy.

Kitchen is to **house** as _____ is to **state**.

○ A. country   B ○. Maine   ○ C. county   ○ D. ranch

Explain how the analogy works: _____

_____

Ready, Set, READ!

Read the passage. Then answer the questions.

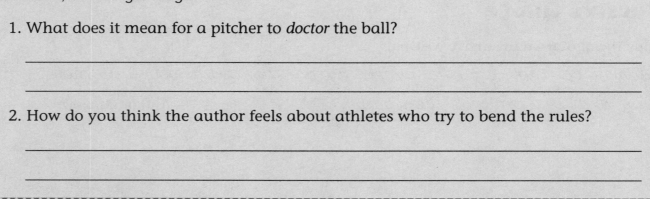

Like most sports, baseball is governed by a strict set of rules to ensure safety and fair play. But like athletes in any sport, some baseball players try to bend the rules to their advantage. Some go further; they cheat. One way that some pitchers cheat is by throwing spitballs.

A "spitter" is a pitch in which the ball is altered by the application of a foreign substance, such as saliva, tobacco spittle, dirt, or petroleum jelly. Doing this changes the aerodynamic properties of the ball, causing it to move differently than it ordinarily would. "Doctoring" the ball also makes it harder to see.

Spitters were once legal and commonplace. They were banned forever after 1920. That was too late for Ray Chapman. During one poorly lit game that season, the unlucky batter was hit in the temple by a spitball thrown by pitcher Carl Mays. Chapman died that night of severe brain trauma.

Although spitballs are illegal, some pitchers still try to alter the ball with lubricants hidden on their uniforms or in their caps. Some even glue sandpaper or pieces of emery board to a finger to scuff the ball. Many are suspected or accused, but few get caught.

1. What does it mean for a pitcher to *doctor* the ball?

_____

_____

2. How do you think the author feels about athletes who try to bend the rules?

_____

_____

⟲ BrainTeaser ⟳

How long a word link can you make?

This word link uses colors:

    yellow → white → eggshell → lavender

Link words by starting a new word with the *last* letter of the word before. Continue the link of country names started below.

Spain → Norway → Yemen →_____

_____

_____

Reading & Math Practice, Grade 6 © 2014 Scholastic Inc.

Number Place

Write each phrase as an algebraic expression.

one less than r _____ n divided by 7 _____

One fourth of y _____ k increased by m _____

the ratio of w and 8 _____   the product of 5 and t _____

You walk a mile in x minutes. How many miles in 60 minutes? _____

Fast Math

Write each percent as a decimal.

40% _____   8% _____   1% _____   11.5% _____

216% _____   0.7% _____   0.3% _____   125% _____

Write each decimal as a percent.

0.2 _____   0.02 _____   0.875 _____   3.5 _____

1.8 _____   0.07 _____   1.25 _____   0.995 _____

Think Tank

A 24-foot flagpole casts a 36-foot shadow. At the same time, Luisa casts a 90-inch shadow. How tall is Luisa?

_____

Show your work in the tank.

Data Place

Box-and-whisker plots show how data is distributed.
This one shows golf scores.

Use the box-and-whisker plot to answer the questions.

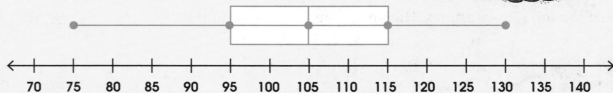

70 75 80 85 90 95 100 105 110 115 120 125 130 135 140

1. What is the upper extreme of the data? _____

2. What is the lowest score any golfer got? _____

3. What is the median of the data? _____

4. What is the median of the upper quartile? _____

5. What is the median of the lower quartile? _____

Puzzler

What percent of the figure is shaded? _____

Reading & Math Practice, Grade 6 © 2014 Scholastic Inc.

WORD of the Day

Use the word below in a short paragraph about a time you stuck with something challenging and saw it through.

persevere: (v.) *keep doing something in spite of difficulties; plug away; persist*

_____

_____

_____

Sentence Mender

Rewrite the sentence to make it correct.

"Do you break for animals! He asked?

_____

Cursive Quote

Copy the quotation in cursive writing.

There is nothing wrong with America that cannot be cured by what is right with America.

—Bill Clinton

_____

_____

_____

What does Clinton mean? Explain. Write your answer in cursive on another sheet of paper.

Analogy of the Day

Complete the analogy.

Cool is to **freezing** as _____ is to **famished**.

○ A. starving   ○ B. stuffed   ○ C. hungry   ○ D. hot

Explain how the analogy works: _____

_____

📖 Ready, Set, READ!

Study the diagram below. It shows a regulation-size tennis court.
Then answer the questions.

1. How far is it from the service
   line to the baseline?

   _____

2. What are the dimensions
   of each backcourt?

   _____

3. What is the area of the
   singles court?

   _____

   The doubles court?

   _____

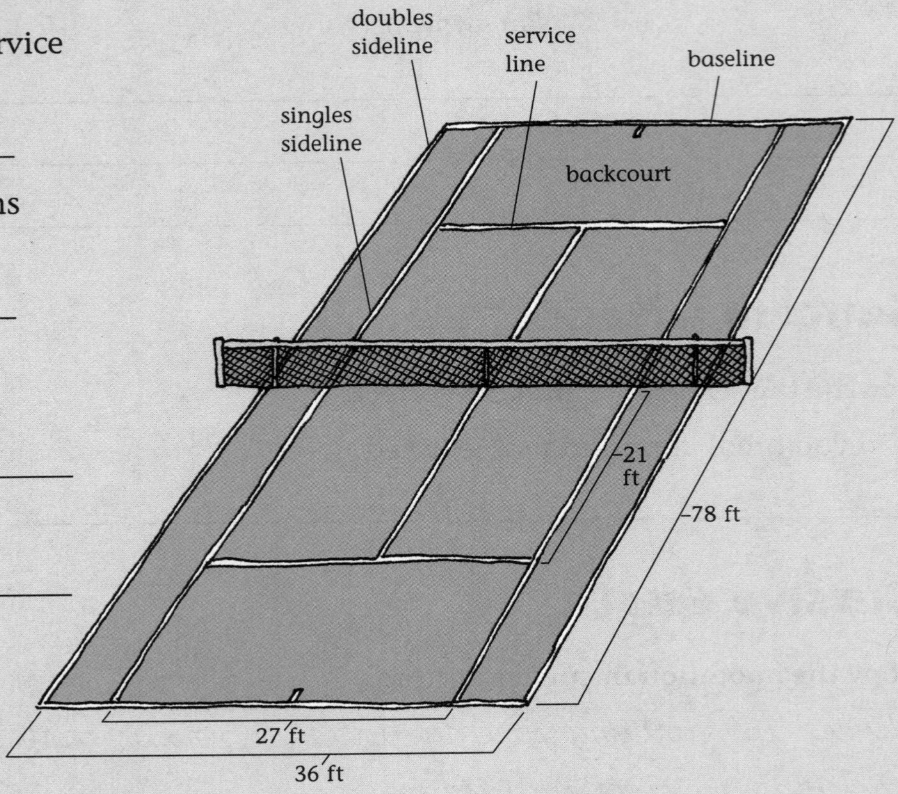

doubles
sideline

service
line

baseline

singles
sideline

backcourt

21
ft

78 ft

27 ft

36 ft

🌀 BrainTeaser 🌀

The table gives two sets of three-letter words. Pick one word from each
column to form a new six-letter word.

Column 1	Column 2	New six-letter word
bar	bid	
bed	her	
don	key	
fat	lam	
for	let	
got	red	
ham	tan	
tar	ten	

Reading & Math Practice, Grade 6 © 2014 Scholastic Inc.

Number Place

Write the opposite of each.

−6 _____   8.5 _____   −3 $\frac{1}{2}$ _____   −0.04 _____

−12 _____   4 $\frac{1}{4}$ _____   −3.5 _____   −1.007 _____

32 _____   53 _____   −3.05 _____   − $\frac{3}{8}$ _____

Fast Math

Find the percent of the number. Use mental math when you can.

20% of 50 _____   15% of 60 _____   50% of 40 _____

12.5% of 64 _____   25% of 8 _____   16 $\frac{2}{3}$ % of 30 _____

Compare. Write **<**, **=**, or **>**.

20% of 20 _____ 25% of 16   62.5% of 40 _____ 83 $\frac{1}{3}$ % of 24

Think Tank

Forty-eight of the 60 members of a chorus sang in the performance. What percent of the chorus did not sing?

_____

Show your work in the tank.

Data Place

When you spin the two spinners together, 12 outcomes are possible.

Use the spinners to answer the questions.

1. Are all 12 outcomes equally likely? _____

2. You spin the spinner at the left. What is the probability that you will spin an even number? _____

3. You spin the spinner at the right. What is the probability that you will spin a number less than 5? _____

You spin both spinners. What is the probability that the following will occur?

4. A 2 and a 5 _____

5. At least one 3 _____

6. Two numbers with a sum of 5 _____

7. Two numbers with a sum of 7 _____

Puzzler

Write *True* or *False*.

1. Any number on a number line is greater than any number to its left. _____

2. The number −6 is to the left of −9 on the number line. _____

3. If x is a positive integer, then $x >$ than 0. _____

4. Any positive integer has a greater absolute value than any negative integer. _____

WORD of the Day

Use the word below in a short paragraph about seeing or creating a copy of something famous.

replica: (n.) *a copy or close reproduction*

_____

_____

_____

Sentence Mender

Rewrite the sentence to make it correct.

Carl found his temper when him brother eve-dropped on his talk with Tina.

_____

Cursive Quote

Copy the quotation in cursive writing.

I suppose leadership at one time meant muscles; but today it means getting along with people.

—Indira Gandhi

_____

_____

_____

What did Gandhi mean by this? Explain. Write your answer in cursive on another sheet of paper.

Analogy of the Day

Complete the analogy.

Key is to **piano** as _____ is to **jacket**.

○ A. shirt   ○ B. pants   ○ C. coat   ○ D. zipper

Explain how the analogy works: _____

_____

📖 Ready, Set, READ!

Read the passage. Then answer the questions.

On October 4, 1957, an event took place that shook the world. That Friday was the day the Russians launched Sputnik 1. Measuring only 22.8 inches in diameter and weighing less than 184 pounds, Sputnik was the first man-made satellite to orbit the earth.

A generation of school children felt its effects. The United States government poured lots of money into schools across the country in an effort to boost math and science education. The space race was on.

American scientists responded to the challenge. The United States claimed victory in 1969, when it landed a crew on the moon. The race was over but technological advances continued. Countless satellites were put in orbit. These have expanded our knowledge of the universe. They have explored every planet in the solar system. They travel beyond it, too, searching for distant galaxies.

Orbiting telescopes are part of the effort. The Hubble Space Telescope is in orbit 380 miles from the earth. It has been sending back incomparable images of the universe. Scientists eagerly look forward to 2018. That's when the James Webb Space Telescope will be launched. It will orbit a *million* miles above the earth! What it may see boggles the imagination.

1. What caused an emphasis on math and science education in the U.S. in 1957?

_____

_____

2. How does the author feel about the future of space exploration?

_____

_____

3. What event marked the end of the space race?

_____

🌀 BrainTeaser 🌀

Long ago, people sent critical messages by telegram. Senders paid by the word, so they attempted to be brief and clear. (Punctuation was free.)

Use the letters below to start each of eight words of a telegram giving valuable information. Add punctuation where it's needed.

V_____   T_____   R_____   O_____

B_____   D_____   S_____   M_____

Number Place

Name the property shown. Write *commutative, associative, identity,* or *distributive.*

4 + 7 = 7 + 4   _____

(3 + 8) + 6 = 3 + (8 + 6)   _____

8 × 1 = 8   _____

–17 + 0 = –17   _____

3 × (8 + 7) = (3 × 8) + (3 × 7)   _____

Fast Math

Find the percent.

What % of 5 is 3? _____   6 is what % of 12? _____

60 is what % of 240? _____   What % of 25 is 20? _____

4.6 is what % of 50? _____   What % of 50 is 125? _____

Think Tank

On a typical day at Curie Middle School 4.5% of the 600 students are absent. How many absences are there in a typical 5-day school week?

_____

Show your work in the tank.

Data Place

Use the figure to answer the questions.

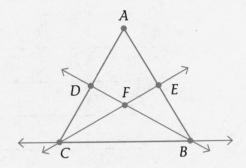

1. Name two lines passing through *F.* _____

2. Name four rays with endpoints at *F.* _____

3. Name three angles with a vertex at *B.* _____

4. Name three angles with a vertex at *D.* _____

5. Name a quadrilateral. _____

6. Name an obtuse triangle. _____

Puzzler

Meg is on one side of a river with her brother, her sister, and a cake. She has to row the kids and the cake across the river. But there's room to take only one thing with her in her small boat. The problem is that she can't leave her brother alone with her sister, nor her sister alone with the cake. Explain how Meg can get everything safely across.

_____

_____

_____

_____

Reading & Math Practice, Grade 6 © 2014 Scholastic Inc.

WORD of the Day

Use the word below in a short paragraph describing something you think is unimportant, but that a friend thinks about a lot.

petty: (adj.) *unimportant; trivial; narrow-minded; secondary in rank*

_____

_____

_____

Sentence Mender

Rewrite the sentence to make it correct.

We leapt out off their seats when the empire yelled "strike three?"

_____

Cursive Quote

Copy the quotation in cursive writing.

Success in life consists of going from one mistake to the next without losing your enthusiasm.

—Winston Churchill

_____

_____

_____

What do you think about this observation? Write your answer in cursive on another sheet of paper.

Analogy of the Day

Complete the analogy.

Defrost is to **warm** as _____ is to **cook**.

○ A. bake   ○ B. eat   ○ C. stove   ○ D. freeze

Explain how the analogy works: _____

_____

📖 Ready, Set, READ!

Read the passage. Then answer the questions.

The first thing you might notice about *manga* is that it reads differently than other comics. Panels go from top to bottom, but you read manga from right to left. This takes some getting used to. But the millions of manga lovers of all ages around the world don't seem to mind.

The term *manga* refers to comics originally published in Japan. It covers genres from action-adventure to comedy, romance, fantasy, horror, and mystery. Manga has been a staple of Japanese magazines for more than a century. Today manga not only represents a large part of Japan's publishing industry, but has gained a worldwide audience. It has had a large effect on comic creators in several countries, including the United States. In Germany, manga-like comics make up three-fourths of all comics sold.

Today's modern form of manga originated in occupied Japan following World War II. It can be described as a blend of traditional Japanese culture and themes and images from American cartoons and television programs. In particular, Disney cartoons have been a key influence. In turn, manga has had a strong impact on the popular Japanese style of animation known as *anime*.

In Japan, manga fans frequent manga cafes. There they drink coffee and read manga to their heart's content. Some enthusiasts even stay overnight!

1. Compare and contrast manga with American comic books.

   _____

   _____

2. What makes manga multicultural? _____

   _____

🌀 BrainTeaser 🌀

Write a funny meaning for each of the made-up words below.
The first one will give you the idea.

1. snorzabaga   <u>sleeping bag for a noisy sleeper</u>_____

2. floration   _____

3. despronk   _____

4. underglam   _____

5. twigshorn   _____

Reading & Math Practice, Grade 6 © 2014 Scholastic Inc.

Number Place

Read the newspaper headlines. Circle the ones that you think have rounded numbers.

- *POPULATION OF BOLIVIA RISES TO 10,000,000*
- *250,000 AT OUTDOOR MUSIC FESTIVAL*
- *32,550 ATTEND STATE FAIR*
- *BANK LOSES $2.45 MILLION IN 3RD QUARTER*
- *CYCLIST CROSSES NATION IN 380 HOURS*

Fast Math

Find the original number.

50% of n is 45 _____

$12\frac{1}{2}$ % of n is 48 _____

550 is 22% of n _____

12 is $16\frac{2}{3}$ % of n _____

18 is 40% of n _____

19% of n is 152 _____

Think Tank

Noah tosses a 1–6 number cube. What is the probability that he will toss a number greater than 2?

_____

What is the probability that he will toss a 7?

_____

Show your work in the tank.

Data Place

You can use more than one type of graph to show the same data. The best graph to use depends upon what it is about the data that you want to show.

Write *bar*, *line*, *circle*, or *histogram* to show what type of graph would be best to show the data described.

1. You want to compare the first month's book sales of two biographies of a famous actor. _____

2. You want to show how your cat spends a typical 24-hour day. _____

3. A rock group just released a new CD. You want to show monthly sales over a 6-month time period. _____

4. You want to show what music people like in their teens, twenties, thirties, and forties. _____

Puzzler

Ross has 6 silver coins that look and feel exactly alike. But one is a fake, and weighs less than the others. Ross has a balance scale. How can he identify the fake coin using only two weighings on the scale? Explain.

_____

_____

_____

_____

Answer Key

Reading 1
Word of the Day: Check the paragraph for accurate usage of the word.
Sentence Mender: Luisa likes our teacher, Mr. Chen, more than I do.
Cursive Quote: Check handwriting for accuracy and legibility. Check that the answer is reasonable.
Analogy of the Day: D; (object-location analogy) Check that the answer is reasonable.
Ready, Set, Read! 1. He was a grumpy, foul-smelling, solitary old man. **2.** *Disparagingly* means in a belittling or disrespectful way. **3.** Old Pete had been a world champion chess player long before the speaker knew him.
Brainteaser: Possible answers: head, herd, here, hire

Math 1
Number Place: (Left to right) 1,352,350; 6,802,387; 2,308,122,050; 19,663,000,000; 7,500,000; 1,005,554,799,000; 499,020,000; 6,999,500,000
Fast Math: 19; 11; 51; 42
Think Tank: 35
Data Place:

Music Group	Tally	Number
Loud Enough	‖‖ ‖‖ ‖	12
Bunny and Hare	‖‖ ‖‖	8
The Bugs	‖‖ ‖‖ ‖‖ ‖‖	20
Squash	‖‖ ‖‖ ‖‖ ‖	16

Puzzler: Answers may vary; sample answer: 358 + 469 + 172

Reading 2
Word of the Day: Check the paragraph for accurate usage of the word.
Sentence Mender: She hopes to win a medal in the track meet.
Cursive Quote: Check handwriting for accuracy and legibility. Check that the answer is reasonable.
Analogy of the Day: B; (synonyms analogy) Check that the answer is reasonable.
Ready, Set, Read! 1. They were probably not educated in science and physics. **2.** *Siphon* means to draw out or empty liquid through a tube or hose.
Brainteaser: 1. crib **2.** crisp **3.** crisis **4.** cringe **5.** critics **6.** crimson **7.** cricket **8.** crinkles

Math 2
Number Place: hundred million; million; ten million; ten billion; billion; hundred million
Fast Math: Answers may vary; sample answers: 9,432 + 657; 7,956 – 423
Think Tank: 4,400 ft²
Data Place: 1. Anchorage **2.** Seattle **3.** Boston
Puzzler: HOSPITAL; POLICE STATION; RAMP CLOSED

Reading 3
Word of the Day: Check the paragraph for accurate usage of the word.
Sentence Mender: Every morning the neighborhood is calm and quiet.
Cursive Quote: Check handwriting for accuracy and legibility. Check that the answer is reasonable.
Analogy of the Day: C; (cause-and-effect analogy) Check that the answer is reasonable.
Ready, Set, Read! 1. The saying means to give away a surprise. **2.** Yes, because the invitation asks guests to bring an appetite. **3.** We don't know the exact date or time of the party. **4.** It asks you to tell the host whether you can come.
Brainteaser: 1. yummy **2.** willow **3.** hearth **4.** ceramic **5.** thrift **6.** oregano **7.** parsnip **8.** earache **9.** rotator **10.** armada

Math 3
Number Place: 300,000,000,010; 59,000,000,130; 606,000,000,000; 32,000,000,000,104
Fast Math: (Left to right) 360; 30,000; 280,000; 49,000; 8,000; 900,000; 48,000; 30,000; 2,800,000; 500,000; 500,000; 10,000
Think Tank: 6 hens
Data Place: 1. ¼ **2.** ⅜ **3.** fantasy and mystery **4.** 18; 17
Puzzler:

387	400	383	391	408
393	405	389	397	385
399	382	395	407	386
409	388	396	384	392
381	394	406	390	398

Reading 4
Word of the Day: Check the paragraph for accurate usage of the word.
Sentence Mender: We should ask our teacher to give less homework on Fridays.
Cursive Quote: Check handwriting for accuracy and legibility. Check that the answer is reasonable.
Analogy of the Day: A; (sequence analogy) Check that the answer is reasonable.
Ready, Set, Read! 1. Immigrants could be denied entry if they had certain diseases. **2.** More than 12 million immigrants entered the United States through Ellis Island.
Brainteaser: 1. ride **2.** vote **3.** peat **4.** table **5.** start **6.** dairy **7.** agree **8.** miles/slime

Math 4
Number Place:

Number	Millions	Thousands	Hundreds
1,700,000	1.7	1,700	17,000
8,000,000	8	8,000	80,000
1,800,000,000	1,800	1,800,000	18,000,000
25,000,000,000	25,000	25,000,000	250,000,000
34,500,000	34.5	34,500	345,000

Fast Math: 9,000; 14,100; 38,100; 68,000
Think Tank: 12 mph; 6 mi
Data Place: 1. Basset EX **2.** Toadster **3.** Toadster, Sloth GT **4.** 65,000 **5.** 97,000
Puzzler: 210 blocks

Reading 5

Word of the Day: Check the paragraph for accurate usage of the word.

Sentence Mender: None of the players on our team speaks Chinese.

Cursive Quote: Check handwriting for accuracy and legibility. Check that the answer is reasonable.

Analogy of the Day: D; (object-location analogy) Check that the answer is reasonable.

Ready, Set, Read! 1. It is a slender, whisker-line organ used to detect taste. **2.** They kill their prey by boring into their bodies, and they release a disgusting gooey slime when frightened.

Brainteaser: Answers may vary; sample answer: Six kicky chicks strike sixty thick, sticky bricks with picks, spikes, and slick sticks.

Math 5

Number Place: (Left to right) 1,000; 1; 10,000,000; 100,000,000; 10,000; 10; 100; 1,000,000

Fast Math: (Left to right) 6,000; 8,000; 25,000; 480,000; 180,000; 600,000

Think Tank: Ike; he has 3 quarters and 4 dimes.

Data Place: 1. 1 h **2.** ¾ h **3.** Wednesday **4.** Thursday; 4¾ h

Puzzler: All answers should be 109,989.

Reading 6

Word of the Day: Check the paragraph for accurate usage of the word.

Sentence Mender: Brian and I are going to the ballgame together tomorrow.

Cursive Quote: Check handwriting for accuracy and legibility. Check that the answer is reasonable.

Analogy of the Day: B; (degree-of-meaning analogy) Check that the answer is reasonable.

Ready, Set, Read! 1. D **2.** B

Brainteaser: Answers will vary; sample answers: **1.** boing **2.** clank **3.** crunch **4.** jangle **5.** rustle **6.** squishes

Math 6

Number Place: (Left to right) 10^2; 10^0; 10^4; 10^6; 10^3; 10^7

Fast Math: (Left to right) 80; 40; 800; 90; 120; 50; >; >

Think Tank: tea

Data Place: 1. Apr. 19, 20, 21, 22, and 23 **2.** Apr. 11, 12, and 13 **3.** Apr. 28 and 29 **4.** Apr. 17, 29 **5.** Apr. 15, 17, 19

Puzzler: The difference between the digits in each number is 4.

Reading 7

Word of the Day: Check the paragraph for accurate usage of the word.

Sentence Mender: The Eiffel Tower is the tallest structure in Paris, France.

Cursive Quote: Check handwriting for accuracy and legibility. Check that the answer is reasonable.

Analogy of the Day: B; (part-whole analogy) Check that the answer is reasonable.

Ready, Set, Read! 1. The writer believes that kids can do their part to help fix up local parks. **2.** The writer got the support of the mayor's office. **3.** It is realistic, optimistic, and upbeat.

Brainteaser: 1. sagas **2.** ewe **3.** civic **4.** Hannah/Elle **5.** repaper

Math 7

Number Place: $(1 \times 10^3) + (5 \times 10^0)$; $(2 \times 10^2) + (1 \times 10^1) + (6 \times 10^0)$; $(4 \times 10^4) + (2 \times 10^3) + (9 \times 10^2) + (6 \times 10^0)$; $(8 \times 10^5) + (4 \times 10^4)$; $(2 \times 10^6) + (7 \times 10^4) + (5 \times 10^3)$; $(3 \times 10^9) + (6 \times 10^8) + (6 \times 10^7)$

Fast Math: (Left to right) Answers may vary; sample answers: 400; 700; 900; 50; 90; 8,000; 90,000; 12; 10,000

Think Tank: 93,499,999 mi

Data Place: 1. 1,156 mi **2.** Chicago and Denver **3.** Denver and Cleveland **4.** 1,478 mi **5.** Detroit and Chicago **6.** Omaha and Denver

Puzzler: 12 kg

Reading 8

Word of the Day: Check the paragraph for accurate usage of the word.

Sentence Mender: People in the northern hemisphere couldn't see the Big Dipper yesterday.

Cursive Quote: Check handwriting for accuracy and legibility. Check that the answer is reasonable.

Analogy of the Day: D; (member-group analogy) Check that the answer is reasonable.

Ready, Set, Read! 1. The climate was affected by the massive amounts of ash thrown into the atmosphere by Tambora, dropping temperatures and diminishing sunlight. **2.** Answers will vary; sample answer: International communication in 1815 was much slower and less comprehensive than it is today.

Brainteaser: 1. wrong song **2.** fake lake **3.** bread spread **4.** swine whine **5.** cross boss **6.** ghoul school

Math 8

Number Place: 90,600; 320,700; 5,409,006; 600,010,080

Fast Math: (Left to right) 169 R31; 1,001; 2,153; 108 R14; 443 R63; 172; 3 R433; 503; 312 R74

Think Tank: 6 + 7 + 8 + 9 = 30

Data Place: 1. (4, 1) **2.** (1, 9) **3.** (9, 1) **4.** (2, 5) **5.** H, Computer City **6.** D, Newsstand **7.** E, Audio Mart **8.** G, Bob's Bakery

Puzzler: A = 2; B = 1; C = 7; D = 8

Reading 9

Word of the Day: Check the paragraph for accurate usage of the word.

Sentence Mender: "Do you have change for a dollar?" she asked.

Cursive Quote: Check handwriting for accuracy and legibility. Check that the answer is reasonable.

Analogy of the Day: C; (degree-of-meaning analogy) Check that the answer is reasonable.

Ready, Set, Read! 1. *Warily* means watchfully, proceeding with great caution. **2.** Answers will vary; sample answer: The adventure was more fun after the ordeal was over than it was during the challenging and scary exploration.

Brainteaser: 1. stunning running **2.** cattle battle **3.** cranky Yankee **4.** melon felon **5.** middle fiddle **6.** better sweater

Math 9

Number Place: <; >; >; =; >; >
Fast Math: 2.2; 100.2; 1.3
Think Tank: 309,649 mi²
Data Place:

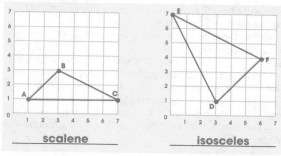

scalene   isosceles

Puzzler:

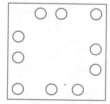

Reading 10

Word of the Day: Check the paragraph for accurate usage of the word.
Sentence Mender: Kelly looked closely at the photo Henry took.
Cursive Quote: Check handwriting for accuracy and legibility. Check that the answer is reasonable.
Analogy of the Day: B; (antonyms analogy) Check that the answer is reasonable.
Ready, Set, Read! 1. Harvey hired Colter to build hotels for travelers on the railroad he worked for. **2.** She was among the few female architects of her time, and worked in very rugged conditions.
Brainteaser: (Top to bottom) fir, hickory, cedar, walnut, hemlock, aspen; forest

Math 10

Number Place: (Left to right) 0.8; 0.06; 0.63; 0.016; 0.0009; 1.02
Fast Math: (Left to right) 15.56; 1.5633; 2.787; 10.3078; 5.9524; 0.165
Think Tank: Rosie makes money; $500
Data Place: 1. 13 **2.** 55 **3.** 95 **4.** Range–45; mean–about 89; median–95; mode–95 **5.** Range–20; mean–about 92; median–95; mode–95
Puzzler: 1. The product of the month's number and the day's number equals the last two digits of the year. **2.** January 12, February 6, and March 4, 2012

Reading 11

Word of the Day: Check the paragraph for accurate usage of the word.
Sentence Mender: We visited the Little Big Horn National Battlefield in southern Montana.
Cursive Quote: Check handwriting for accuracy and legibility. Check that the answer is reasonable.
Analogy of the Day: A; (object-function analogy) Check that the answer is reasonable.
Ready, Set, Read! 1. A **2.** D **3.** C
Brainteaser: 1. disown **2.** qualms **3.** resourceful **4.** difficult **5.** phony **6.** utmost **7.** endurance **8.** parrot

Math 11

Number Place: $y = 0.4$; $w = 0.7$
Fast Math: (Left to right) 8; 63; 10; 80; 20; 40; 90; 60
Think Tank: 39 in; 3,281 ft
Data Place:

Quarter	1	2	3	4	Final Score
Bees	3	6	10	8	27
Moths	3	7	2	14	26

Puzzler: 10

Reading 12

Word of the Day: Check the paragraph for accurate usage of the word.
Sentence Mender: In every town people have disagreements over raising taxes.
Cursive Quote: Check handwriting for accuracy and legibility. Check that the answer is reasonable.
Analogy of the Day: A; (example-class analogy) Check that the answer is reasonable.
Ready, Set, Read! 1. He was asked to build a special ride for the 1893 World Columbian Exposition in Chicago. **2.** They provided six stops during the first revolution so terrified riders could get off.
Brainteaser:

Math 12

Number Place: 0.00012; 60.09; 0.0047; 7,000.022
Fast Math: (Left to right) 0.2; 0.63; 4; 20; 0.07; 3; 3,024; 504.7
Think Tank: 6.45 oz
Data Place: 21.5 mpg
Puzzler:

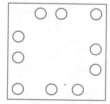

Reading 13

Word of the Day: Check the paragraph for accurate usage of the word.
Sentence Mender: The burial took place at the cemetery on Thursday.
Cursive Quote: Check handwriting for accuracy and legibility. Check that the answer is reasonable.
Analogy of the Day: D; (object-description analogy) Check that the answer is reasonable.
Ready, Set, Read! Answers will vary; sample answers: **1.** Some people believe that humans then had neither the interest nor technological know-how. **2.** The author sides with the scientists, that these ancient structures were indeed made by people.
Brainteaser: 1. angel, angle **2.** strap, traps **3.** baker, break **4.** elbow, below **5.** horse, shore **6.** stain, satin

Math 13

Number Place:

Number	Nearest 1,000	Nearest 100,000
389,900	390,000	400,000
1,844,938	1,845,000	1,800,000
24,061,562	24,062,000	24,100,000

Fast Math: 0.0017; 0.6; 2.198; 2,370
Think Tank: 38,292.4 miles
Data Place: 1. 6.3 oz **2.** 9.8 oz **3.** croquet **4.** no **5.** table tennis ball
Puzzler: 162; 4; 40; no, there will be two leftover students.

Reading 14

Word of the Day: Check the paragraph for accurate usage of the word.
Sentence Mender: We descended the stairs rapidly during the fire drill.
Cursive Quote: Check handwriting for accuracy and legibility. Check that the answer is reasonable.
Analogy of the Day: B; (object-location analogy) Check that the answer is reasonable.
Ready, Set, Read! 1. Heels lifted them above the filth in the streets. **2.** Answers will vary; sample answer: He wanted to ensure that he was taller than his nobles.
Brainteaser:

Word	1 thing	2 or more	Can't tell
1. goose	✓		
2. mice		✓	
3. radio	✓		
4. women		✓	
5. scissors			✓
6. grapefruit			✓
7. headquarters			✓
8. cattle		✓	

Math 14

Number Place: (Left to right) 30,900,000; 92,807.05; 1,286,000.4; 4,000,041,000; 8,726,739.03; 5,528,910,000
Fast Math: (Left to right) 800; 156; 1.9; 0.625; <; >; >
Think Tank: 57.6 ft
Data Place: Sample graph:

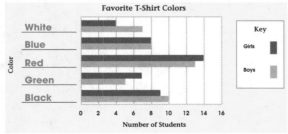

Answers will vary; sample answer: In general, the difference between the colors that boys and girls chose is not very great.
Puzzler: Biscuit; all Finn's preferred foods end in consonants.

Reading 15

Word of the Day: Check the paragraph for accurate usage of the word.
Sentence Mender: We saw a scrawny kitten that needed food badly.
Cursive Quote: Check handwriting for accuracy and legibility. Check that the answer is reasonable.
Analogy of the Day: A; (cause-and-effect analogy) Check that the answer is reasonable.
Ready, Set, Read! 1. Very little; we know him mostly through his connection with many classic fables. **2.** Answers will vary; sample answer: The author values the fables themselves far more than the background of their creator.
Brainteaser: 1. cello **2.** bassoon **3.** clarinet **4.** marimba **5.** piccolo **6.** mandolin **7.** ukelele **8.** accordion **9.** saxophone **10.** harmonica

Math 15

Number Place: (Left to right) 0.05; 10; 0.009; 40; 7,000; 0.005
Fast Math: 0.03; 0.011; 0.15; 25
Think Tank: 9.12 km
Data Place:

Player	Hits	At-bats	Batting Average
Jackson	5	40	.125
Ruiz	27	90	.300
Morita	46	184	.250
Hunter	48	120	.400
Sullivan	26	60	.433

1. Morita **2.** Hunter **3.** 9
Puzzler: 1. 137 – 84 **2.** 78 × 43 + 1 **3.** 48 × 371

Reading 16

Word of the Day: Check the paragraph for accurate usage of the word.
Sentence Mender: Do you see a doctor regularly?
Cursive Quote: Check handwriting for accuracy and legibility. Check that the answer is reasonable.
Analogy of the Day: D; (part-whole analogy) Check that the answer is reasonable.
Ready, Set, Read! 1. If you aren't pushing yourself hard, you may see no benefits. **2.** Walking is low impact; it requires no special preparation, training, or equipment. **3.** It feels natural, it doesn't hurt, you can breathe easily.
Brainteaser: Answers will vary; sample answers:

	C	O	R	D
Sports	cycling	orienteering	rugby	dodgeball
Birds	canary	oriole	robin	dove
States	California	Oregon	Rhode Island	Delaware
Rivers	Columbia	Ohio	Roanoke	Danube

Math 16

Number Place: 0.6834; 124.755
Fast Math: (Left to right) 7; 1; 8; 9; 7; 45
Think Tank: 7.249 m
Data Place: 1. 5 **2.** 4 **3.** 1 **4.** 11
Puzzler:

1.   2.

Reading & Math Practice, Grade 6 © 2014 Scholastic Inc.

Reading 17

Word of the Day: Check the paragraph for accurate usage of the word.
Sentence Mender: The baseball team's co-captains, Carlos and Kim, are hitting like Babe Ruth.
Cursive Quote: Check handwriting for accuracy and legibility. Check that the answer is reasonable.
Analogy of the Day: D; (example-class analogy) Check that the answer is reasonable.
Ready, Set, Read! 1. He looked forward to finding out when he'd be taken fishing. **2.** Answers will vary; sample answer: It sounds bittersweet.
Brainteaser: 1. lei **2.** prey **3.** decay **4.** weigh **5.** buffet **6.** cliche (or cliché) **7.** matinee **8.** Pompeii

Math 17

Number Place: (Left to right) 8; 5; 6; 3; 1; 13; 12 and 18; there are none.
Fast Math: (Left to right) 9; 3; 13; 3; 8; 0
Think Tank: 2 7/8 lb
Data Place: 1. 80 **2.** Wednesday and Thursday **3.** 235 **4.** They are declining. **5.** Answers may vary; sample answers: A new pizza store opened nearby; there was bad weather.
Puzzler:

$1\frac{2}{3}$	$\frac{3}{4}$	$1\frac{1}{6}$	$1\frac{7}{12}$
$1\frac{1}{2}$	$1\frac{1}{4}$	$\frac{2}{3}$	$1\frac{3}{4}$
$\frac{11}{12}$	$1\frac{5}{6}$	$1\frac{5}{12}$	1
$1\frac{1}{12}$	$1\frac{1}{3}$	$1\frac{11}{12}$	$\frac{5}{6}$

Reading 18

Word of the Day: Check the paragraph for accurate usage of the word.
Sentence Mender: "Hey! Come back this minute, you rascal," yelled Jed.
Cursive Quote: Check handwriting for accuracy and legibility. Check that the answer is reasonable.
Analogy of the Day: B; (object-action analogy) Check that the answer is reasonable.
Ready, Set, Read! 1. Hydroponics is the science of growing plants in nutrient-enriched water, but without soil. **2.** Answers will vary; sample answer: The writer never told the kind of plant chosen, or what specific nutrients were added. **3.** The plant grown hydroponically grew best.
Brainteaser: Answers will vary; check word list.

Math 18

Number Place: (Left to right) 12; 10; 80; 60; 60; 360; 56; 135; 104
Fast Math: (Left to right) $\frac{1}{2}$; $\frac{7}{12}$; 7 3/8; 3/40; 1 7/8; 2 3/4; 1 23/24; 28 11/18
Think Tank: Greater than; as terms increase and the difference stays the same, the value of the fraction increases.
Data Place: 1. 1 **2.** 8 **3.** 2 **4.** 36–40; it is the tallest bar.
Puzzler: 1. 12.56, 1.08 **2.** 31.2, 19.4 **3.** 15.5, 2.5

Reading 19

Word of the Day: Check the paragraph for accurate usage of the word.
Sentence Mender: If you want something done, ask a busy person.
Cursive Quote: Check handwriting for accuracy and legibility. Check that the answer is reasonable.
Analogy of the Day: C; (object-function analogy) Check that the answer is reasonable.
Ready, Set, Read! Answers will vary; sample answers:
1. Royals had leisure time; they may not have believed that the laws applied to them; they had vast estates on which to play.
2. *Unprofitable* means having no clear advantage or benefit.
Brainteaser: 1. aroma **2.** teapot **3.** widow **4.** cleric **5.** noggin **6.** overdo **7.** pickup **8.** render **9.** surpass

Math 19

Number Place: (Left to right) 0; 1; $\frac{1}{2}$; $\frac{1}{2}$; 0; $\frac{1}{2}$; $\frac{1}{2}$; $\frac{1}{2}$; answers may vary; sample answers: 5/11; 7/15; 9/18; 5/9; 13/27; 4/8; 10/21; 15/30
Fast Math: (Left to right) $\frac{1}{2}$; $\frac{1}{6}$; 12; 14 2/3; 50; 1 1/4
Think Tank: 19 1/8 ft^3
Data Place: 1. $14.00 **2.** No; she'll be $1.40 short. **3.** Tadpole Taco with special pond sauce, 1 drink, 1 dessert
Puzzler: 66 handshakes

Reading 20

Word of the Day: Check the paragraph for accurate usage of the word.
Sentence Mender: My friend won the essay contest, but to me, Fran's piece was the best.
Cursive Quote: Check handwriting for accuracy and legibility. Check that the answer is reasonable.
Analogy of the Day: B; (object-description analogy) Check that the answer is reasonable.
Ready, Set, Read! Answers will vary; sample answers:
1. He taught women at a time when this practice was forbidden. **2.** Both the scarcity of written records and the passage of time make it difficult for historians to reconstruct many ancient events.
Brainteaser: 1. lima **2.** limp **3.** limbs **4.** limit **5.** limber **6.** limerick **7.** limestone **8.** limousine

Math 20

Number Place: (Left to right) 100; 10,000; 1,100; 3,000; 1,000,000; 10,025
Fast Math: (Left to right) 13 1/3; 9 1/2; 32; 5; 6 1/4; 8,000; <; =; =; <; <; <
Think Tank: 1½ min
Data Place: 1. 48 **2.** 6 **3.** 15/48 or 5/16 **4.** 36/48 or 3/4 **5.** fourth and seventh
Puzzler: Pair off numbers to make sums of 101; 101 × 50 = 5,050

Reading 21

Word of the Day: Check the paragraph for accurate usage of the word.
Sentence Mender: Swamps, marshes, and bogs are all wetlands. Note: the series comma before *and* is optional.
Cursive Quote: Check handwriting for accuracy and legibility. Check that the answer is reasonable.
Analogy of the Day: A; (example-class analogy) Check that the answer is reasonable.
Ready, Set, Read! 1. He never came across any monsters at sea. **2.** Sample answer: It took centuries and advances in technology to accurately map the world's vast seas.
Brainteaser: 1. band **2.** medal **3.** bizarre **4.** sealing **5.** currant **6.** whether **7.** assistants

Reading & Math Practice, Grade 6 © 2014 Scholastic Inc.

Math 21

Number Place: 5,999,999,998; 1,000,499,999
Fast Math: (Left to right) 0.06; 9,700; 480; 19,000; 768; 0.621; =; >; >; >; =; >
Think Tank: City A because 145 cm > 139.5 cm
Data Place: **1.** 9.4; $32.81 **2.** 19.3; $59.64 **3.** $29.53
Puzzler: The stack would reach about one mile in height.

Reading 22

Word of the Day: Check the paragraph for accurate usage of the word.
Sentence Mender: I think it was Elena who left her backpack on the bus.
Cursive Quote: Check handwriting for accuracy and legibility. Check that the answer is reasonable.
Analogy of the Day: A; (sequence analogy) Check that the answer is reasonable.
Ready, Set, Read! **1.** C **2.** B **3.** She could see everything clearly.
Brainteaser: (Top to bottom) **1.** sapphire **2.** garnet **3.** topaz **4.** emerald **5.** jade; diamond

Math 22

Number Place: >; <; >; >
Fast Math: (Left to right) 2; 4; 2; 1; $1\frac{1}{20}$; $\frac{5}{8}$; $\frac{2}{3}$; 4; $\frac{6}{11}$
Think Tank: $333\frac{1}{3}$ pounds
Data Place: **1.** $6.68 **2.** $7.06
Puzzler: **1.** 7 **2.** 11

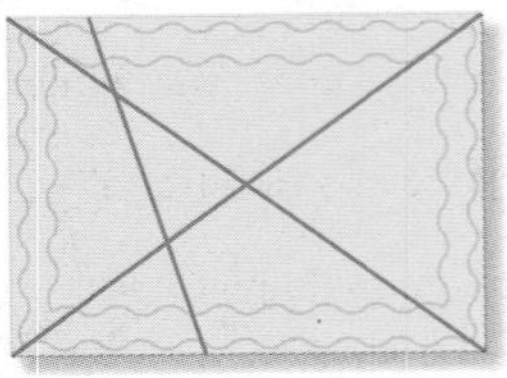
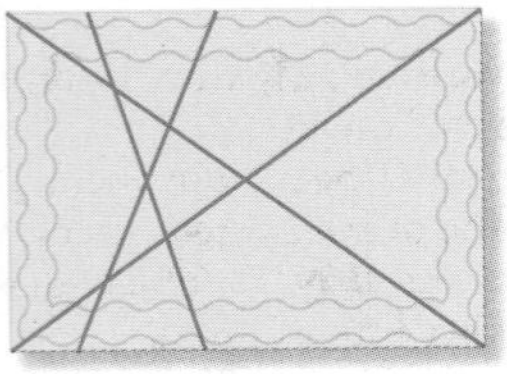

Reading 23

Word of the Day: Check the paragraph for accurate usage of the word.
Sentence Mender: Hey! What are you doing with my laptop?
Cursive Quote: Check handwriting for accuracy and legibility. Check that the answer is reasonable.
Analogy of the Day: D; (synonyms analogy) Check that the answer is reasonable.
Ready, Set, Read! **1.** You need a mixing bowl, measuring cup, fork, skillet, and spatula. **2.** You'd need 8 eggs. 3. the toppings
Brainteaser: **1.** pines/snipe; **2.** plane **3.** verse/veers/serve **4.** master **5.** caller **6.** itself **7.** antler **8.** remote

Math 23

Number Place: Answers may vary; sample answers: $3y$; $7b$; $m - 6$; $\frac{w}{4}$; $p + 10$
Fast Math: (Left to right) 21; 45; $\frac{1}{90}$; 16; $10\frac{1}{2}$; $2\frac{2}{3}$; $2\frac{1}{6}$; $2\frac{2}{5}$; 4
Think Tank: 63
Data Place: **1.** I, II, III **2.** (1, 6), (5, −2), (6, 2) **3.** Boxer, IV
Puzzler: Answers may vary; sample answer:

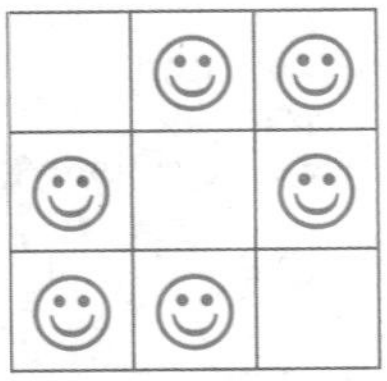

Reading 24

Word of the Day: Check the paragraph for accurate usage of the word.
Sentence Mender: The coach sees that he needs to have the players practice more often.
Cursive Quote: Check handwriting for accuracy and legibility. Check that the answer is reasonable.
Analogy of the Day: C; (member-group analogy) Check that the answer is reasonable.
Ready, Set, Read! **1.** Sideburns are patches of facial hair grown on the side of the face near the ears. **2.** Sample answer: The photo proves how thick and bushy his side whiskers were, and how they connect by the moustache.
Brainteaser: **1.** minute **2.** advance **3.** exclude **4.** sameness **5.** mourn **6.** increase **7.** develop **8.** serious

Math 24

Number Place: $x = 0.3$; $z = 1.85$
Fast Math: (Left to right) 11, 8, 8, 8; 34, 60, 59, no mode
Think Tank: range = 12; mean = about 89; median = 90; mode = 90
Data Place:

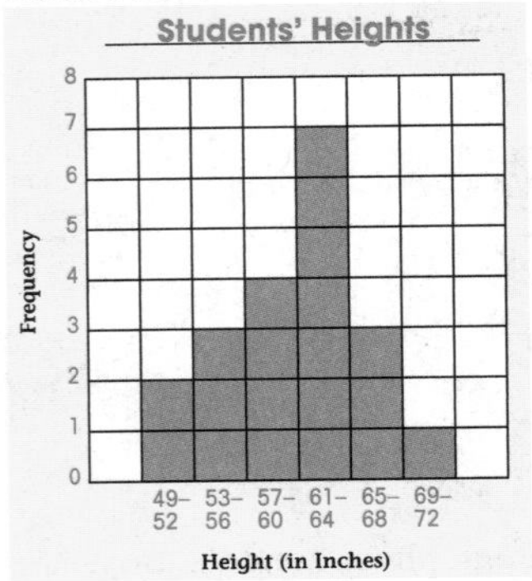

Puzzler: 3.7 + 4.6 = 8.3; 1.9 + 3.0 = 4.9; 2.3 + 4.9 = 7.2

Reading 25

Word of the Day: Check the paragraph for accurate usage of the word.
Sentence Mender: The Taj Mahal in India may be the world's most famous tomb.
Cursive Quote: Check handwriting for accuracy and legibility. Check that the answer is reasonable.
Analogy of the Day: B; (object-function analogy) Check that the answer is reasonable.
Ready, Set, Read! Answers will vary; sample answers: **1.** How many different kinds of stains did you try to remove? **2.** Does it remove ALL stains in seconds? **3.** Who gave you these quotations, and did anyone have a negative reaction?
Brainteaser: The nine-letter word is carpetbag; check word list for acceptable and correctly spelled words.

Math 25

Number Place: −6, −4; −8, −2
Fast Math: (Left to right) $.88, $2.42, $2.35, $2.35; $2\frac{7}{8}$, $1\frac{27}{40}$, $1\frac{1}{8}$, no mode
Think Tank: 296–297
Data Place: **1.** F **2.** D **3.** C **4.** B **5.** D
Puzzler: The 7-lb bag has tea.

Reading 26

Word of the Day: Check the paragraph for accurate usage of the word.

Sentence Mender: The Lindsay twins look alike but don't think alike.

Cursive Quote: Check handwriting for accuracy and legibility. Check that the answer is reasonable.

Analogy of the Day: D; (antonyms analogy) Check that the answer is reasonable.

Ready, Set, Read! 1. They built a railroad to connect the east and west coasts of America. **2.** They faced difficult terrain, massive obstacles, and long hours of grueling work.
3. *Transcontinental* means across the continent.

Brainteaser: 1. equal **2.** clique **3.** squash **4.** liquid **5.** racquet **6.** frequent **7.** eloquent **8.** tranquil

Math 26

Number Place: −5; +400; −75; +6

Fast Math: $n + 7$; $n − 2.8$; $n^2 + 8$; $12n$

Think Tank: $40.00

Data Place: Questions will vary; sample questions: **1.** On which two days did Mia run a total of 7 km? **2.** How much farther did Mia run on Monday than on Sunday? **3.** What is the difference between her longest and shortest runs?

Puzzler: The line segment is a chord crossing from between 9 and 10 to between 3 and 4. The sum on each side of the chord is 39.

Reading 27

Word of the Day: Check the paragraph for accurate usage of the word.

Sentence Mender: Working one on one with a math tutor was very helpful.

Cursive Quote: Check handwriting for accuracy and legibility. Check that the answer is reasonable.

Analogy of the Day: B; (sequence analogy) Check that the answer is reasonable.

Ready, Set, Read! 1. A calabash is a kind of gourd; when dried out, it can serve as a dipper or cup. **2.** Answers will vary; sample answer: Every person's contribution counts.

Brainteaser: 1. pennant **2.** ballpark **3.** outfield **4.** playoffs **5.** shutout **6.** sacrifice **7.** division **8.** statistic **9.** reliever **10.** league

Math 27

Number Place: $n > 3$; $n \geq −2$

Fast Math: $2n + 3$; $3n − 4^2$; $2n − 5$; $2.5n + 8.5$; $45n^2$

Think Tank: $10 + d$

Data Place:

Sneaker Size	Tally	Frequency
5	I	1
7	I	1
8	⊬⊬	5
9	⊬⊬ I	6
10	IIII	4
11	IIII	4
12	III	3
14	I	1

Summaries will vary.

Puzzler: 9

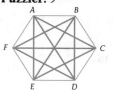

Reading 28

Word of the Day: Check the paragraph for accurate usage of the word.

Sentence Mender: Both she and I missed the deadline for reports, and it hurt our grades.

Cursive Quote: Check handwriting for accuracy and legibility. Check that the answer is reasonable.

Analogy of the Day: C; (object-description analogy) Check that the answer is reasonable.

Ready, Set, Read! Answers will vary; sample answers: **1.** The speaker longs for peace and serenity. **2.** He uses metaphors in verse 2; he uses vivid images of nature to evoke the serenity of the place.

Brainteaser: (Top to bottom) twenty, death, away; they went dataway

Math 28

Number Place: $m \geq −1$; $m < −4$

Fast Math: (Left to right) 7; 22; 3; 14; 1; 11; 27.5; 4; 5

Think Tank: $145.5/y$

Data Place: Sample graph:

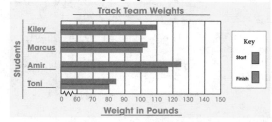

1. Find the greatest difference between start and finish weights.
2. For each person, divide the total weight lost by the start weight. The greatest quotient matches the person who had lost the greatest fraction of his or her start weight.

Puzzler:

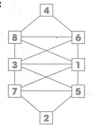

Reading & Math Practice, Grade 6 © 2014 Scholastic Inc.

Reading 29

Word of the Day: Check the paragraph for accurate usage of the word.
Sentence Mender: Monica opened the window this morning and looked out.
Cursive Quote: Check handwriting for accuracy and legibility. Check that the answer is reasonable.
Analogy of the Day: A; (part-whole analogy) Check that the answer is reasonable.
Ready, Set, Read! 1. Flores was a Philippine immigrant who popularized the yo-yo in the United States in the 1920s. **2.** An ancient Greek bowl shows a boy playing with a yo-yo. **3.** Answers will vary.
Brainteaser: 2. basket **3.** spray **4.** night **5.** bank **6.** ink

Math 29

Number Place: (Left to right) 0.9; $\frac{6}{100}$; $\frac{10}{1,000}$; 0.05; 1.003; $-4\frac{1}{100}$; $-1\frac{4}{1,000}$; $2\frac{3}{10,000}$
Fast Math: (Left to right) 10.81; 5.62; 0.61; 6.37; 3.24; 0.89
Think Tank: Tuesday
Data Place: 1. 3:30 P.M., 5:30 P.M., 6:30 P.M. **2.** 4:00 A.M., 6:00 A.M., 5:00 A.M. **3.** 8:15 P.M., 5:15 P.M., 7:15 P.M.
Puzzler:

Reading 30

Word of the Day: Check the paragraph for accurate usage of the word.
Sentence Mender: Right after my birthday, I sent out thank-you notes.
Cursive Quote: Check handwriting for accuracy and legibility. Check that the answer is reasonable.
Analogy of the Day: D; (object-user analogy) Check that the answer is reasonable.
Ready, Set, Read! 1. Both were female artists who painted landscapes of the part of the world they loved; both succeeded against great odds. **2.** *Indigenous* means born and raised in a certain area. **3.** Answers will vary; sample answer: An artist might prefer solitary time to observe, meditate, plan, and create without outside interferences or distractions.
Brainteaser: 1. badgers **2.** daggers **3.** dangers **4.** gardens **5.** grasped **6.** regards **7.** sugared

Math 30

Number Place: -9, -6, -5, -2; -40, -4, 4, 40; 19, 9, -9, -91; 17, 7, -17, -77
Fast Math: (Left to right) $5n$; $3n$; $7n$; $7n - 3s$; $9y + 2$; $12t$
Think Tank: $60
Data Place:

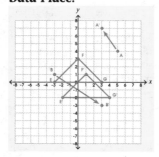

1. $A'(3, 7)$; $B'(3, -3)$
2. translation: down 2 units, right 1 unit
Puzzler: $31.20

Reading 31

Word of the Day: Check the paragraph for accurate usage of the word.
Sentence Mender: Many of us realize that soda, candy, and junk food are bad for our health. Note: the series comma before *and* is optional.
Cursive Quote: Check handwriting for accuracy and legibility. Check that the answer is reasonable.
Analogy of the Day: C; (cause-and-effect analogy) Check that the answer is reasonable.
Ready, Set, Read! 1. Answers will vary. **2.** Answers will vary; sample answer: The author thinks that Thorpe should have gotten the recognition he earned.
Brainteaser: Answers will vary; check adjectives.

Math 31

Number Place: (Left to right) $\frac{12}{20}$, $\frac{5}{20}$; $\frac{9}{10}$, $\frac{4}{10}$; $\frac{35}{60}$, $\frac{36}{60}$; $<$; $<$; $=$
Fast Math: $w + 2.5 = 3.8$; $y - 82 = 47$; $\frac{7}{0.5} = 2$; $\frac{3}{8}k = 1\frac{7}{8}$
Think Tank: 180 miles
Data Place: 1. 23 **2.** 21 **3.** 8 stories **4.** between 11 and 22 **5.** 22 stories
Puzzler: 1. $\frac{9}{21}$; any fraction $= \frac{3}{8}$ **2.** $1\frac{11}{18}$; any number equivalent to $1\frac{5}{9}$

Reading 32

Word of the Day: Check the paragraph for accurate usage of the word.
Sentence Mender: "Climate" and "weather" are two terms that are often confused.
Cursive Quote: Check handwriting for accuracy and legibility. Check that the answer is reasonable.
Analogy of the Day: B; (example-class analogy) Check that the answer is reasonable.
Ready, Set, Read! 1. The Newbery Award is given annually to the author who has written the best children's book of the year. **2.** Answers will vary; sample answer: Reading Engle's exact words shows her motivations for writing and her desire to inspire readers.
Brainteaser: Answers will vary; check verbs.

Math 32

Number Place: $\frac{5}{8}$, $\frac{5}{6}$, $\frac{6}{7}$, $\frac{7}{8}$; $\frac{3}{10}$, $\frac{3}{8}$, $\frac{1}{2}$, $\frac{3}{5}$; $\frac{10}{7}$, $1\frac{1}{7}$, 1, $\frac{7}{10}$; $2\frac{3}{4}$, $2\frac{2}{3}$, $2\frac{1}{2}$, $2\frac{2}{5}$
Fast Math: (Left to right) $n = 135$; $m = 16$; $b = 99$; $y = 13$; $t = 14$; $n = 311$
Think Tank: 14 bugs
Data Place: 1. Wynn Field, 48,000 **2.** Clark Park **3.** Wynn Field **4.** Clark Park **5.** 11,280
Puzzler: Perimeter = 32 units; Area = 64 square units

Reading 33

Word of the Day: Check the paragraph for accurate usage of the word.
Sentence Mender: "There are cougar tracks ahead, so be careful," the ranger warned.
Cursive Quote: Check handwriting for accuracy and legibility. Check that the answer is reasonable.
Analogy of the Day: A; (antonyms analogy) Check that the answer is reasonable.
Ready, Set, Read! 1. Joao knows he will be out of town too much to take on the responsibility. **2.** It is friendly. **3.** It means that he feels too out of practice, or possibly out of shape, to do the job.
Brainteaser: Answers will vary; sample answer: Restless, rowdy, rampaging rogue rhinoceroses rumpled rare, royal robes.

Reading & Math Practice, Grade 6 © 2014 Scholastic Inc.

Math 33
Number Place: (Left to right) <; =; >; >; >; =
Fast Math: (Left to right) $n = 20$; $w = 15$; $y = 13,800$; $s = 1,800$; $m = 2.5$; $p = 8,450$
Think Tank: Multiply the weekly price by 52. Find the difference between the two total prices to determine the savings.
Data Place:

Quarter	1	2	3	4	Final Score
Modem	10	5	17	9	41
Drive	7	9	13	14	43

The Drive
Puzzler:

Reading 34
Word of the Day: Check the paragraph for accurate usage of the word.
Sentence Mender: Buying a good dictionary may be the wisest investment a writer can make.
Cursive Quote: Check handwriting for accuracy and legibility. Check that the answer is reasonable.
Analogy of the Day: C; (degree-of-meaning analogy) Check that the answer is reasonable.
Ready, Set, Read! 1. A *horse of a different color* means something that might seem similar at first, but is actually quite different. **2.** Answers will vary; sample answer: In hard times, audiences were looking for cheap entertainment while contestants sought the chance to win prize money. **3.** It was sad to watch desperate, exhausted dancers hoping to outlast other pairs.
Brainteaser: Answers may vary; sample answers: sandy, sands, sends, bends, beads, heads, hears

Math 34
Number Place: (Left to right) <; >; >; <; <; >
Fast Math: (Left to right) $n = 1.2$; $m = 26$; $b = 2.36$; $y = 50$; $t = 3.4$; $r = 0.1017$
Think Tank: $3,382\frac{1}{2}$ ft³
Data Place: 1. yes **2.** The horizontal scale has been expanded in Graph B. **3.** Graph A
Puzzler: $3\frac{1}{4} + 5\frac{5}{8} = 9$

Reading 35
Word of the Day: Check the paragraph for accurate usage of the word.
Sentence Mender: This morning, wearing my pajamas, I ate an egg.
Cursive Quote: Check handwriting for accuracy and legibility. Check that the answer is reasonable.
Analogy of the Day: B; (synonyms analogy) Check that the answer is reasonable.
Ready, Set, Read! 1. Sample answer: The saying means to make the wrong choice or follow the wrong course; examples will vary. **2.** D
Brainteaser: (Top to bottom) 7, 8, 6, 1, 4, 3, 9, 5, 2

Math 35
Number Place: (Top to bottom) −1.6, −1.2, 1.2, 1.6; −1½, −½, ½, 1; −10.01, −10, 10.1; −2¼, −2, 2, 2¼
Fast Math: (Left to right) $n = 1\frac{7}{10}$; $m = \frac{5}{8}$; $b = \frac{13}{14}$; $y = 7\frac{3}{8}$; $t = 1\frac{2}{5}$; $k = 2\frac{1}{2}$
Think Tank: 10; 55
Data Place: 1. 3 **2.** 2 **3.** 69 **4.** 26 **5.** 54 **6.** 7
Puzzler: 47

Reading 36
Word of the Day: Check the paragraph for accurate usage of the word.
Sentence Mender: My pal's name is hard to spell because she is from Wales.
Cursive Quote: Check handwriting for accuracy and legibility. Check that the answer is reasonable.
Analogy of the Day: C; (example-class analogy) Check that the answer is reasonable.
Ready, Set, Read! 1. B **2.** A
Brainteaser: (Top to bottom) crania, tact; Antarctica

Math 36
Number Place: 400, 85, 145,405; 92, 164, 65,408; 330, 132, 12,408
Fast Math: (Left to right) $n = 152$; $m = 18\frac{2}{3}$; $b = 1\frac{1}{8}$; $w = \frac{4}{7}$; $t = 2\frac{1}{12}$; $p = 10$
Think Tank: ⅑
Data Place:

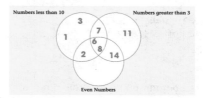

Puzzler:

Reading 37
Word of the Day: Check the paragraph for accurate usage of the word.
Sentence Mender: Please keep this secret between the two of us.
Cursive Quote: Check handwriting for accuracy and legibility. Check that the answer is reasonable.
Analogy of the Day: D; (example-class analogy) Check that the answer is reasonable.
Ready, Set, Read! 1. The reviewer finds this movie exciting, entertaining, visually interesting, and gripping. **2.** Answers will vary; sample answer: The reviewer names famous directors and characters to link this movie with great high-tech adventure classics. **3.** The reviewer is suggesting that the movie is so exciting, it might help to sit with a calm person for balance.
Brainteaser: Answers will vary; check word list.

Math 37
Number Place: (Left to right) 3, 9; 2, 5, 10; 2, 3, 4, 6, 8; 2, 3, 5, 6, 9, 10; 2, 3, 4, 5, 6, 10
Fast Math: (Left to right) 5; −2; 4; 10; 0; −15; −4; −8; −4
Think Tank: 14 ft²
Data Place:

Stem	Leaf
4	7
5	4 5 9 9
6	2 2 2 6
7	0 3
8	2 2

1. 35 **2.** 62 **3.** 62 **4.** median
Puzzler: The answer should be the original integer.

Reading 38

Word of the Day: Check the paragraph for accurate usage of the word.
Sentence Mender: We have seen amazing photos of Jupiter's moons.
Cursive Quote: Check handwriting for accuracy and legibility. Check that the answer is reasonable.
Analogy of the Day: C; (object-description analogy) Check that the answer is reasonable.
Ready, Set, Read! 1. They believed that bathing was a mark of how civilized they were. **2.** Cretan bathrooms had sloped floors and no running water.
Brainteaser: (Top to bottom) ate, tear, rates, stared, roasted, roadster, costarred

Math 38

Number Place: c, p, c, p, p; false, 2 is an even prime number; false, 2 + 3 = 5
Fast Math: (Left to right) 8; −40; 126; −250; 0; 96; −40; 48; −42
Think Tank: −1°C
Data Place: 1. mean, 69.3 **2.** mode, 90 **3.** median, 63
Puzzler: 1. no; figure would have > 180° **2.** yes **3.** yes **4.** no; figure would have < 360°

Reading 39

Word of the Day: Check the paragraph for accurate usage of the word.
Sentence Mender: "Yes, we went to the famous zoo when we visited San Diego," said Li's aunt.
Cursive Quote: Check handwriting for accuracy and legibility. Check that the answer is reasonable.
Analogy of the Day: D; (antonyms analogy) Check that the answer is reasonable.
Ready, Set, Read! 1. The songwriter loves the clear, quiet, peaceful, open spaces of the range. 2. Sample answer: He feels how small he is in the great universe around him, and wonders what might be on those stars.
Brainteaser:

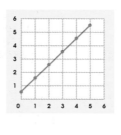

Math 39

Number Place: (Left to right) 326; 15; 18; 4.5; ⅖; 0.6; 22; 0; 87; ⅝
Fast Math: (Left to right) 5½; 1⅜; 5⅓; 1¼; 0; −9; −4.7; −⅖; 1/12
Think Tank: 0.5 days
Data Place:

x	x + 0.5	(x, y)
0	0.5	(0, 0.5)
1	1.5	(1, 1.5)
2	2.5	(2, 2.5)
3	3.5	(3, 3.5)
4	4.5	(4, 4.5)
5	5.5	(5, 5.5)

1. yes **2.** The graph is a straight line.
Puzzler: 7:00; 1:30; 9:25

Reading 40

Word of the Day: Check the paragraph for accurate usage of the word.
Sentence Mender: My friend and I saw a collection of thirty-seven fossils at a museum.
Cursive Quote: Check handwriting for accuracy and legibility. Check that the answer is reasonable.
Analogy of the Day: A; (object-function analogy) Check that the answer is reasonable.
Ready, Set, Read! 1. Answers and explanations will vary.
2. Sample answer: Optimists see people as basically good and life as fair and joyful, while pessimists have a negative, darker view.
Brainteaser: 1. volleyball **2.** embarrass **3.** wheelbarrow **4.** penniless **5.** fuzzballs **6.** buccaneer **7.** cassette **8.** occurred

Math 40

Number Place: (Left to right) $2^3 = 8$; $2^2 \times 3^3 = 108$; $3^4 \times 4 = 324$; $5^3 \times 12 = 1,500$; $3^2 \times 4^3 = 576$; $6^2 \times 2^2 = 144$
Fast Math: Answers may vary; (left to right) any number > 9; any number < −21; any number < −5; any number ≤ −1; any number > 2; any number ≤ −4
Think Tank: 1:50 A.M.
Data Place: 1. Negative correlation; the temperature drops as the time gets later. **2.** 4:00 P.M. to 8:00 P.M.
Puzzler: 40

Reading 41

Word of the Day: Check the paragraph for accurate usage of the word.
Sentence Mender: I bought a roundtrip ticket on the 3 o'clock train to Santa Fe, New Mexico.
Cursive Quote: Check handwriting for accuracy and legibility. Check that the answer is reasonable.
Analogy of the Day: B; (object-user analogy) Check that the answer is reasonable.
Ready, Set, Read! 1. They couldn't be shipped without refrigeration. **2.** Answers and explanations will vary; sample answer: The banana had its start in Malaysia but was then brought to many different countries around the world.
Brainteaser: 1. Halfway—then he's on the way out! **2.** yesterday, today, tomorrow **3.** charcoal

Math 41

Number Place: (Left to right) <; >; =; >; >; <; >; >; <
Fast Math: (Left to right) 1 to 3; 2 : 5; ⅓; 2 to 3; 5 : 3; 2 to 1; 4 : 1; ⅐; 3 to 5; 2 : 1
Think Tank: 4 to 3; 4 to 9
Data Place: 1. 20% **2.** 28% **3.** 68% **4.** 100% **5.** 76% **6.** 140%
Puzzler:

Reading & Math Practice, Grade 6 © 2014 Scholastic Inc.

Reading 42

Word of the Day: Check the paragraph for accurate usage of the word.

Sentence Mender: Galileo was a scientist whose ideas were not accepted during his lifetime.

Cursive Quote: Check handwriting for accuracy and legibility. Check that the answer is reasonable.

Analogy of the Day: C; (object-location analogy) Check that the answer is reasonable.

Ready, Set, Read! 1. The better she knows the person, the greater the gift. **2.** *Go whole hog* means to put on a complete show.

Brainteaser:

Name	Room	Game
Kita	kitchen	pinball
Paco	den	Tetris
Ted'	study	Neopets

Math 42

Number Place: (Left to right) 2^3; 2^5; 5^3; 2×5^2; $2^2 \times 3 \times 5$; $2^5 \times 3$

Fast Math: (Top to bottom) 9 to 6, 36 : 24; 20 : 14, 1 to 0.7; 9 to 5; (left to right) ≠; =; =; ≠; =; =

Think Tank: 12

Data Place:

Item	Gil's Grocery	Mira's Market	Fiona's Foods
Corn Muffin	4 for $6	10 for $18	5 for **$7.40**
Yogurt	4 for $3.40	6 for $4.62	5 for **$3.75**
Canned Tuna	6 for $7.50	4 for $4.88	5 for **$6.00**

Puzzler:

Object	Top View	Front View	Side View

Reading 43

Word of the Day: Check the paragraph for accurate usage of the word.

Sentence Mender: John Woo, the director, will have a film showing at the festival next year.

Cursive Quote: Check handwriting for accuracy and legibility. Check that the answer is reasonable.

Analogy of the Day: B; (object-function analogy) Check that the answer is reasonable.

Ready, Set, Read! 1. D **2.** C

Brainteaser: 2. baby bottle **3.** cookie cutter **4.** Freaky Friday **5.** helping hands **6.** green giant **7.** time travel **8.** Secret Service **9.** cut corners **10.** night nurse

Math 43

Number Place: Answers will vary; sample answers: (left to right) ²⁄₄, ⁴⁄₈; ⁶⁄₁₀, ⁹⁄₁₅; −⁶⁄₁₆, −⁹⁄₂₄; 1 ²⁄₄, 1 ¹⁰⁄₂₀; −3 ⁴⁄₁₀, −3 ⁸⁄₂₀; 5 ⁸⁄₂₀, 5 ⁹⁄₃₀; −²⁄₈, −³⁄₁₂; −⁴⁄₁₄, −⁶⁄₂₁; −3 ¹⁴⁄₁₆, −3 ²¹⁄₂₄

Fast Math: (Left to right) 7 mph; 1 for $7; 8 ft/sec; 1 for $3.50; 1.5 pages/min; 1 can for $.60

Think Tank: 600 doses

Data Place:

Player	Years	Won	Lost
Lefty Lebowitz	1988–1990	42	14
Hands Hansen	1997–1999	**48**	16
Stringbean Gomez	2004–2006	36	**12**
Baby Face Jonas	2008–2010	**33**	11
Big Mo Tanaka	2012–	15	**5**

18 games

Puzzler: (Top to bottom)

Reading 44

Word of the Day: Check the paragraph for accurate usage of the word.

Sentence Mender: Those roses were the prettiest flowers I'd ever seen.

Cursive Quote: Check handwriting for accuracy and legibility. Check that the answer is reasonable.

Analogy of the Day: D; (synonyms analogy) Check that the answer is reasonable.

Ready, Set, Read! 1. They hoped to retrieve the body, or at least keep the fish from eating it. **2.** *Festooned* means decorated with.

Brainteaser:

H	E	A	R	T
E	M	B	E	R
A	B	U	S	E
R	E	S	I	N
T	R	E	N	D

Math 44

Number Place: (Left to right) ½; ⁴⁄₅; ⅙; −⁴⁄₇; −⁵⁄₈; −²⁄₉; −⅕; 1 ¾; 1 ²⁄₅; −2 ⁷⁄₉

Fast Math: (Left to right) yes; no; no; no; yes; yes; no; no; yes

Think Tank: 7 ft

Data Place: Answers may vary; sample answers: **1.** 1 circle to 2 triangles **2.** 2 triangles to total number of figures **3.** 1 circle to 6 polygons **4.** 3 quadrilaterals to 1 hexagon **5.** 2 triangles to 3 quadrilaterals

Puzzler:

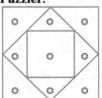

Reading 45

Word of the Day: Check the paragraph for accurate usage of the word.

Sentence Mender: We sat around the kitchen table and spoke about Dad's exciting news.

Cursive Quote: Check handwriting for accuracy and legibility. Check that the answer is reasonable.

Analogy of the Day: D; (example-class analogy) Check that the answer is reasonable.

Ready, Set, Read! 1. Sangheeta argues that same-sex classes would benefit sixth graders in many ways. **2.** Answers will vary; sample answer: Sangheeta's views sound like opinions, though they may have some basis in her personal experience.

Brainteaser: 1. line **2.** tank **3.** make **4.** bill **5.** on

Math 45

Number Place: (Left to right) $1\frac{5}{7}$; $2\frac{2}{3}$; $-2\frac{2}{3}$; $4\frac{1}{2}$; $-1\frac{2}{3}$; $-\frac{5}{4}$; $\frac{67}{20}$; $\frac{22}{9}$; $\frac{19}{3}$; $-\frac{29}{13}$

Fast Math: (Left to right) 15; 3; 13; 2; 56; 30; 36; 14; 3

Think Tank: 6 in

Data Place: 1. $75 **2.** January **3.** $79 **4.** March

Puzzler:

Object	Top View	Front View	Side View

Reading 46

Word of the Day: Check the paragraph for accurate usage of the word.

Sentence Mender: All my buddies showed up for my party last night.

Cursive Quote: Check handwriting for accuracy and legibility. Check that the answer is reasonable.

Analogy of the Day: A; (object-location analogy) Check that the answer is reasonable.

Ready, Set, Read! 1. C **2.** B

Brainteaser: Sample answers: **1.** weight **2.** prejudice **3.** envelope **4.** none **5.** granted **6.** keep **7.** flesh **8.** safe **9.** time **10.** call

Math 46

Number Place: (Left to right) -0.7; $-\frac{3}{50}$; $\frac{1}{25}$; -0.03; -7.8; $-44\frac{11}{20}$; $-\frac{7}{500}$; 61.125

Fast Math: (Left to right) $\frac{7}{10}$; $\frac{1}{20}$; $\frac{16}{25}$; $1\frac{1}{2}$; $\frac{19}{20}$; $2\frac{1}{4}$; $\frac{3}{25}$; $1\frac{6}{25}$; 40%; 87.5%; 80%; 62.5%; 160%; 4%; 7%; 125%

Think Tank: 6 cm

Data Place: 1. 32% **2.** 16% **3.** 40% **4.** 12% **5.** 40% **6.** 76%

Puzzler: Player 1

Reading 47

Word of the Day: Check the paragraph for accurate usage of the word.

Sentence Mender: Isn't Carla older than her brother's friend?

Cursive Quote: Check handwriting for accuracy and legibility. Check that the answer is reasonable.

Analogy of the Day: C; (part-whole analogy) Check that the answer is reasonable.

Ready, Set, Read! 1. It means to disfigure or alter the ball in some way that makes it harder for the batter to hit. **2.** Answers may vary; sample answer: The author seems to view this practice with distaste and provides dramatic evidence of its sad consequences.

Brainteaser: Answers will vary; sample answer: New Zealand, Denmark, Kenya, Austria . . .

Math 47

Number Place: (Left to right) $r - 1$; $\frac{7}{7}$; $\frac{1}{4}y$ or $\frac{y}{4}$; $k + m$; $\frac{7}{8}$; $5t$; $\frac{60}{x}$

Fast Math: (Left to right) 0.4; 0.08; 0.01; 0.115; 2.16; 0.007; 0.003; 1.25; 20%; 2%; 87.5%; 350%; 180%; 7%; 125%; 99.5%

Think Tank: 60 in or 5 ft tall

Data Place: 1. 130 **2.** 75 **3.** 105 **4.** 115 **5.** 95

Puzzler: 31.25%

Reading 48

Word of the Day: Check the paragraph for accurate usage of the word.

Sentence Mender: "Do you brake for animals?" he asked.

Cursive Quote: Check handwriting for accuracy and legibility. Check that the answer is reasonable.

Analogy of the Day: C; (degree of meaning analogy) Check that the answer is reasonable.

Ready, Set, Read! 1. 18 ft **2.** 18 ft x 27 ft **3.** 27 x 78 = 2,106 sq ft; 36 x 78 = 2,808 sq ft

Brainteaser: Order may vary: barred, bedlam, donkey, father, forbid, gotten, hamlet, tartan

Math 48

Number Place: (Left to right) 6; -8.5; $3\frac{1}{2}$; 0.04; 12; $-4\frac{1}{4}$; 3.5; 1.007; -32; -53; 3.05; $\frac{3}{8}$

Fast Math: (Left to right) 10; 9; 20; 8; 2; 5; $=$, $>$

Think Tank: 20%

Data Place: 1. yes **2.** $\frac{1}{2}$ **3.** $\frac{2}{3}$ **4.** $\frac{1}{12}$ **5.** $\frac{7}{12}$ **6.** $\frac{1}{6}$ **7.** $\frac{1}{6}$

Puzzler: 1. T **2.** F **3.** T **4.** F

Reading 49

Word of the Day: Check the paragraph for accurate usage of the word.

Sentence Mender: Carl lost his temper when his brother eavesdropped on his talk with Tina.

Cursive Quote: Check handwriting for accuracy and legibility. Check that the answer is reasonable.

Analogy of the Day: D; (part-whole analogy) Check that the answer is reasonable.

Ready, Set, Read! 1. Americans wanted to keep pace with Russian scientific advances. **2.** Sample answer: The author maintains optimism and excitement about future discoveries. **3.** The event that ended the space race was the U.S. moon landing.

Brainteaser: Answers will vary; sample telegram: Violent tornado ravages Omaha! Buildings destroyed, scores missing!

Math 49

Number Place: commutative; associative; identity; identity; distributive

Fast Math: (Left to right) 60%; 50%; 25%; 80%; 9.2%; 250%

Think Tank: 135

Data Place: 1. *DB, CE* **2.** *FE, FB, FC, FD* **3.** Answers may vary; sample answers: *EBF, FBC, EBC* **4.** Answers may vary; sample answers: *BDC, ADB, ADC* **5.** *ADFE* **6.** *CFB*

Puzzler: Answers may vary; sample answer: Cross first with sister; leave her there; return for brother; leave brother and bring back sister; drop off sister, pick up cake, take it across and leave it with brother; go back to bring sister across.

Word of the Day: Check the paragraph for accurate usage of the word.

Sentence Mender: We leapt out of our seats when the umpire yelled, "Strike three!"

Cursive Quote: Check handwriting for accuracy and legibility. Check that the answer is reasonable.

Analogy of the Day: A; (cause-and-effect analogy) Check that the answer is reasonable.

Ready, Set, Read! 1. Sample answer: Both tell stories through drawing and few words; manga is read from right to left rather than left to right. **2.** Manga combined traditional Japanese themes with modern American images, and there are now manga-like comics in many countries.

Brainteaser: Answers will vary; sample answers: **2.** covering a flat surface completely with flowers **3.** to unwrap the springs inside a mechanical device **4.** to intentionally dress poorly **5.** description of shrubs after they have been closely pruned

Math 50

Number Place: Answers may vary; sample answers: (top to bottom) rounded; rounded; exact; exact; exact

Fast Math: (Left to right) 90; 72; 384; 45; 2,500; 800

Think Tank: $\frac{2}{3}$; 0

Data Place: Answers may vary; sample answers: **1.** bar **2.** circle **3.** line **4.** histogram

Puzzler: Step 1: Put three coins in each pan to weigh them. Step 2: Weigh any two coins from the lighter pan. The fake coin is the lighter coin; if the pans are in balance, the fake is the third coin.

You can use this page to work out your answers.